Simone de Beauvoir

Photo by Henri Cartier-Bresson

Simone de Beauvoir: Encounters with Death

Elaine Marks

RUTGERS UNIVERSITY PRESS
New Brunswick, New Jersey

Library of Congress Cataloging in Publication Data

Marks, Elaine.
Simone de Beauvoir: encounters with death.

Includes bibliographical references.
1. Death—Psychology. 2. Beauvoir, Simone de,
1908–   I. Title.
BF789.D4M37   194   72–4199
ISBN 0-8135-0707-3

To Gabriel and in memory of Sidonia

Contents

Preface

Lengthy quotations from Simone de Beauvoir's writings open most of the chapters of this book. They are intended to make the book self-sufficient and to enable the reader to follow the argument more easily. The physical distance between the text and comment is thus considerably reduced. The translations that are not followed by an English title are mine, except in the case of *Les Belles Images*, whose English edition carries the same French title. The French texts and quotations for each chapter have been placed at the back of the book. I have used, in their literal English translation, three terms frequently found in French existentialist jargon: "the other," "bad faith," and "scandal." "The other," *l'autre*, refers to other people envisaged as the enemy; "bad faith," *la mauvaise foi*, describes an attempt at dissimulating the real nature of one's relations with the world; "scandal," *le scandale*, often translated as "original evil," refers particularly to that aspect of human experience which is most unacceptable and unbearable, death.

I should like to thank Simone de Beauvoir, who generously allowed me to read and to quote from two unpublished typed manuscripts: the sixty-three pages originally intended to be a first chapter of *L'Invitée*, which relate the childhood of Françoise Miquel, and the two hundred and eighty-two pages of the five *récits* that form "La Primauté du spirituel."

Acknowledgments of financial and spiritual aid are gratefully made to the Institute for Research in the Humanities of the University of Wisconsin.

Simone de Beauvoir

Je connais que pauvres et riches,
Sages et fous, prêtres et lais,
Nobles, villains, larges et chiches,
Petits et grands, et beaux et laids,
Dames à rebrassés collets,
De quelconque condition,
Portant atours et bourrelets,
Mort saisit sans exception.
　　　—François Villon, *Le Grand Testament*

CHAPTER I

Death and Sensibility

Simone de Beauvoir is one of the most significant writers of the twentieth century and one of the most popular writers of her generation in France and abroad. Her significance and her popularity are intimately related. Simone de Beauvoir always writes about or around the major preoccupation of the modern sensibility, the preoccupation with death, and she does this in a manner that reaches a wide and varied audience.

The modern sensibility explicitly or implicitly involves the death of God. It comprehends both the feeling of emptiness at the heart of all things, more commonly referred to as the sense of the absurd, and a desperate need to fill the emptiness, more commonly referred to as commitment. Each of these domains has in its literary manifestations particular themes and modes of description.

The absurd is explored from a metaphysical and an aesthetic point of view by those indefatigably lucid writers whose ethic is to awaken the somnambulists, to demystify the believers, and to shatter the screens that mask the human condition as it is and things in the world as they are. Two simple but terrifying images describe this vision: a human being agonizing on a bed; a human being attempting to stand upright as the planet whirls in space.

The desperate need to fill the emptiness, the need for commitment, has its own vision and its own aesthetic. Its goal is to change the reader and ultimately the world through the transformation of human consciousness. Man is seen as historical rather than as mortal. The collectivity has a direction, a purpose; there is a discernible process and pattern in its becoming. Commitment involves a belief and believers with an ardent spirit of seriousness. The endless repetitions and patterns of the absurd are replaced by movement and activity. The rhythm of commitment is busy and regulated. Its tone, concerned, humorless, optimistic, is never ironic; its language, rhetorical and oracular, is solemn, full of confidence and conviction. The major theme is unity and the point of view is always moral, social, and political.

Gratuity, the monarch in the universe of the absurd, is replaced by usefulness, play by total activity, analysis by synthesis, phenomenology by ideology. In the leap from the absurd to commitment, from death to history, a concrete problem is given abstract answers. A curtain is drawn around the bed and the planet is suddenly immobile.

Both visions, both aesthetics, are present in the writings of Simone de Beauvoir. There is a constant dialectic between the fear of death and the dread of nothingness, the feeling of impotence and failure and the robust, energetic vigor of an optimistic believer who is at the same time a sincere witness and a merciless judge. These correspond to radical stylistic changes: moments of heightened intensity, rigorous descriptions of sensations and sentiments; pitiless and poignant analyses of weaknesses follow or are followed by an often mediocre, vulgar journalese in which endless explanations of the obvious and simpering moralistic clichés annoy and embarrass the reader. Death and the absurd are always more elegant and refined than history and commitment. There is never a synthesis of the two domains. They remain distinct because the relation between them is unexplored and unresolved. The superiority of Simone de Beauvoir's style when she writes about death and the absurd reveals her fundamental obsession.

This study concentrates on the crucial element of her sensibility: encounters with death. The manner in which these encounters arise, the feelings they elicit, the role accorded these feelings, and the ways of escaping them tell us a great deal about the modern dilemma: the refusal to confront what is known. Encounters with death need not involve an actual death. The fear of death, feelings towards death, illness, anguish, eroticism, and the horror of the other are different forms of encounters, equally valid in terms of sensibility.

Some of the greatest scenes in the literature of the nineteenth and twentieth centuries are scenes of encounters with death. The number and quality of these encounters substantiate the claim of their importance. Many of them utilize the basic image of someone agonizing on a bed; the death of Old Goriot, the death of Madame Bovary, the death of Ivan Ilych, the deaths of Oscar and Antoine Thibault, the death of the narrator's (Marcel's) grandmother, the death of Vergil, the death of Malone. Still other works are pervaded by the presence of death, are indeed encounters with death from the first page to the last: *Heart of Darkness*, *Death in Venice*, *The Dead*, *Finnegans Wake*, *The Diary of a Country Priest*, *As I Lay Dying*, *A Death in the Family*, *The Stranger*, *Death in Midsummer*, the complete works of Dostoyevsky, the diaries and letters of Cesare Pavese, the poetry of Stéphane Mallarmé and Yves Bonnefoy. The difference between these literary *danses macabres* and those of preceding centuries is that until the nineteenth century death was generally viewed as the fulfilling of a destiny, sacred or human. Death was aesthetically the proper end for a metaphor. Death was a relief and an acceptance, a beginning as well as an end. Death was the source of beauty and art, attempts to perpetuate what is doomed and therefore precious. From the nineteenth century on, death is more and more often presented as inacceptable, an inhuman "scandal." What used to evoke sighs and tears is now intended to evoke screams and vertigo. There is no beginning; only a skull and a gaping hole. Death is the brutal and the ubiquitous mystery, a private as well as a collective obsession.

All the books written by Simone de Beauvoir—memoirs, novels, *récits*, her one play, essays, *reportage*—are concerned with the emptiness at the heart of all things which underline the last words of the third volume of her memoirs, "I was gypped," and defiant attempts to overcome this emptiness. Each encounter with death is followed by a leap into history and commitment—either to a cause or to others—each commitment is followed by an encounter with death which each time, as if for the first time, is a shattering fall. From the unpublished manuscript of "La Primauté du spirituel" to the last published essay, *La Vieillesse*, Simone de Beauvoir and her characters leap and fall with amazing resiliency and intense suffering. In general the fictional works contain more falls, the essays more leaps. With the publication of *Les Mandarins* in 1954 the leaps decrease and the encounters with death become more frequent and are more lucidly, doggedly confronted. It is not by accident that Simone de Beauvoir's best work, the first volume and the end of the third volume of her memoirs and *Une Mort très douce*, involve encounters with death: the death of God, the death of her friend Zaza, the projection of her death and Sartre's, the death of her mother. There is no passage to awareness in Simone de Beauvoir's world that does not involve death.

The major encounters with death, except for the death of her mother, play a role in more than one work: the confrontation with the old jacket in the unpublished *récit* on the childhood of Françoise Miquel, in *L'Invitée*, *Le Sang des autres*, the *Mémoires d'une jeune fille rangée*, with thematic echoes in *Tous les Hommes sont mortels*, *L'Existentialisme et la sagesse des nations*, *Les Mandarins*, *La Force de l'âge;* the death of Louise's baby in *Le Sang des autres*, *Pyrrhus et Cinéas*, the *Mémoires d'une jeune fille rangée;* the death of Zaza in the unpublished *récits* of "La Primauté du spirituel" and in the memoirs; death during the occupation in *Le Sang des autres*, *Les Bouches inutiles*, *Les Mandarins*, and the memoirs; old age as a prelude to death in the memoirs, *Une Mort très douce*, *Les Belles Images*, *La Femme rompue*, and *La Vieillesse*. There are also, in the memoirs, minor encounters, insistent reminders, persistent sorrows: the death of her father, of Boris Vian, of her secretary Lucienne Baudin, of Albert Camus, of Merleau-Ponty. Nor are the essays, whatever their topic, immune to the preoccupation with death.

Beyond these major and minor encounters there is *the* encounter which furnishes the impetus for Simone de Beauvoir's creative power and the entire network of themes and images she elaborates in her fiction and nonfiction. *The* encounter is a constant presence, the presence of the self engaged in a losing combat to preserve itself from annihilation and from the intrusion of others. Death for Simone de Beauvoir is nothingness, absence. The length of most of her books, the interminable descriptions and lists in the memoirs as well as in her studies on the United States and China and the refusal to cut or trim words, sentences, and experiences can be explained by the obsession with death. To expurgate is to kill the self, to reduce it to oblivion. Things written down, both the facts of life and the feelings that accompany them, are a bulwark for the living against the inevitable end. Simone de Beauvoir writes to consolidate the past and the present; to ward off the future.

The titles of many of her works from *L'Invitée* to *La Vieillesse* refer explicitly or implicitly to death. In *L'Invitée* it is the guest, "the other," who annihilates the protagonist Françoise, who obliges her to kill in order not to be killed. The presence of "the other" is a constant reminder of the imminent death of the self. In *Pyrrhus et Cinéas*, Pyrrhus is the man of action who proposes goals to be achieved here and now; Cinéas, the nonbeliever, is the nihilist who continues to ask why, given man's finite, mortal condition, he should go to so much trouble. In *Le Sang des autres* it is again "the other," the other for whom the narrator feels responsible, whom his actions affect and kill. In *Les Bouches inutiles* the old and the infirm, the women and the children are threatened with collective death. In *Tous les Hommes sont mortels*, it is the fact of mortality that gives meaning to human lives; Fosca, immortal, is inhuman, he no longer partakes of the human, mortal, sensibility. In *Pour une morale de l'ambiguïté*, ambiguity is a consequence of mortality, which is the essential fact and a fundamental category of all experience. In *L'Amérique au jour le jour* the hectic rhythm of Simone de Beauvoir's daily adventure in the United States is a form of supreme *divertissement*, a long flight from the anguish and the deaths she had recently experienced in Occupied France. In *L'Existentialisme et la sagesse des nations*, the commonplaces through which we see the world protect us from real encounters. In *Le Deuxième Sexe*, oppressed women, like all oppressed groups, are maintained in a state of bondage, again incapable of real encounters. In *Les Mandarins*, a group of French intellectuals attempt to grapple with the fundamental life-death enigma in postwar Paris. In *Privilèges* death becomes the alibi of the man of "bad faith," the bourgeois, his excuse for refusing history. In the memoirs, the life of Simone de Beauvoir is presented in detail and chronologically against a background of recurrent encounters with death. Memoirs involve time and death; they are an attempt to save the fabric of her life from death. In *Une Mort très douce*, the "scandal" of every death is slowly documented as Simone de Beauvoir watches her mother, dying of cancer, watch herself die. In *Les Belles Images*, sadness and death are systematically rejected in favor of more palatable fictions. In the three *récits* of *La Femme rompue*, the voices of three broken women speak of old age, failure, and death, physiological and psychological death. In *La Vieillesse* dying and death are the indispensable facts. What the titles reveal, beyond the insistent concern with death, is the progressive intensity and specificity of this preoccupation as Simone de Beauvoir grows older.

A significant number of Simone de Beauvoir's works begin with an anecdote, an experience, or a quotation that immediately involves the reader with death and nothingness. In the *récit* on the childhood of Françoise Miquel, in *L'Invitée*, *Pyrrhus et Cinéas*, *Tous les Hommes sont mortels*, *Pour une morale de l'ambiguïté*, and *La Vieillesse*, the opening pages or paragraphs are microcosms of the author's obsession.

Simone de Beauvoir tends to use in her fiction stock characters, who reappear from work to work in similar configurations and who are, for the most part, easily traceable to the characters and the relationships between them that exist in the memoirs. These stock characters, who all appear for the first time in *L'Invitée*, can perhaps best be defined and differentiated by their attitude towards death. The young girl, revolted, absolutist, who challenges the seriousness of the protagonist's project—Xavière in *L'Invitée*, Hélène in *Le Sang des autres*, Clarisse in *Les Bouches inutiles*, Béatrice in *Tous les Hommes sont mortels*, Nadine in *Les Mandarins*—has occasional seizures of metaphysical anguish. Her anguish, however, because of her age, is easily distracted by sexual encounters. Whereas the older women, aged thirty and beyond, whether they are the heroines—Françoise in *L'Invitée*, Catherine in *Les Bouches inutiles*, Régine in *Tous les Hommes sont mortels*, Anne in *Les Mandarins*, Laurence in *Les Belles Images*, André's wife in "L'Age de discrétion"—or the ladies of "bad faith," Elisabeth in *L'Invitée*, Denise in *Le Sang des autres*, Paule in *Les Mandarins*, the narrators of the *récits* "Monologue" and "La Femme rompue" are all subject to severe, nearly fatal bouts of anguish. In contrast, the leading male characters—(with the exception of Denis in "Marguerite" and Fosca in *Tous les Hommes sont mortels*) Pierre in *L'Invitée*, Louis in *Les Bouches inutiles*, Jean in *Le Sang des autres*, Henri and particularly Dubreuil in *Les Mandarins*, André in "L'Age de discrétion"—are curiously impervious to any form of anguish that is not related to a specific situation. The reason for this male-female dichotomy is simple: all the male characters work constantly at a project which absorbs and distracts them. The women, even those who, like the heroines, work, are never totally immersed in what they do. What they lack is the ambition to succeed, which, closely linked to personal vanity, plays a greater role in conditioning the sensibility of the male characters than either metaphysical revery or affairs of the heart. In the world of Simone de Beauvoir—and in startling contrast to her conclusions at the end of *Le Deuxième Sexe*—it is the women of all ages who persistently come up against the emptiness at the heart of all things in their relations to others and to the world. The following conversation between the male and female protagonists of *Le Sang des autres* is revealing:

"How can we find within ourselves good reasons for living, since we die?"

"That makes no difference."

"I think it makes all the difference." She stared at me with curiosity. "Don't you mind thinking that some day you'll not be here, and that there'll not even be anyone to think of you?"

"If I've lived my life as I wanted, what does it matter?"

"But for a life to be interesting it must be like going up in an elevator; you come to one floor, then another, then another, and each floor is only there because of the floor above it." She shrugged her shoulders. "So, if once you get to the top, everything falls to pieces— it's just ridiculous from the start, don't you think so?"

"No," I said absentmindedly.[1]

Precisely because the men do not let themselves go metaphysically or psychologically they are particularly attractive to the often hysterical women, who, in different ways, all repeat Régine's cry to Fosca in *Tous les Hommes sont mortels:* " 'Save me,' she said. 'Save me from death.' "[2]

Place as well as character bears a definite relation to death. Simone de Beauvoir's natural habitat is Paris. She has a Parisian sensibility in the sense that Paul Valéry or Albert Camus may be said to have a Mediterranean sensibility. She has been conditioned by an allegretto Parisian tempo which she, in turn, imposes on everything she creates.

The stuffy left-bank apartments of her youth, the small left-bank hotel rooms of the war years from which she escaped to the left-bank cafés and small nightclubs, the studio on the Rue Schoelecher—("When I went to sleep for the first time in my new room, I thought: 'This is the bed I shall die in' ")[3]—the streets filled with demonstrators constitute the basic elements of her left-bank Parisian decor. "I spent the first twenty years of my life in a big village that stretched from the Lion de Belfort to the Rue Jacob, from the Boulevard Saint-Germain to the Boulevard Raspail: I still live there." [4] Despite her many voyages Simone de Beauvoir and her characters always return to this same Paris. The apartments, hotels, cafés, streets and boulevards of which she writes exist: the Boulevard Montparnasse, the Hôtel Royale Bretagne, the Rue de la Gaîté, the Hôtel du Danemark, the Rue Vavin, the Rue Dauphine, le Dôme, le Hoggar, la Coupole, le Select, le Jockey, la Flore, les Deux Maggots. These are real places in a real city, but they are also projections of Simone de Beauvoir's inner, obsessive world.

The apartments and hotel rooms she describes suggest an enclosed, solitary universe at whose center is the bed on which she is afraid of dying, alone, and from which she is impelled to flee to the streets, the cafés, the railroad stations, to crowds, movements, nature, and above all to words. Paris, her Paris, is a city of words: verbal constructions proliferate, are destroyed and created anew. "One night in June, 1944, I tried to exorcise death with words. I excerpt some of my notes here, just as they came from my pen." [5] All Simone de Beauvoir's writings may be seen as a desperate effort to "exorcise death with words." The major female characters she presents also attempt to exorcise death with words, and they exist in a place which is itself under the double sign of death and the word.

CHAPTER II

The Old Jacket: Intimations of Nothingness

The house was empty, the blinds had been drawn to shut out the sun and it was dark; on the first floor landing Françoise was standing flat against the wall holding her breath. The stairs and the old floor slats had creaked and the windows of the library shook a little; now there was no noise at all. The door of my room, the bathroom door, grandmother's room, daddy's and mother's room. It was funny to be there all alone when everyone else was in the garden; it was funny and frightening; the furniture looked just as it always did, but at the same time it was completely changed; thick and heavy and secret; under the bookcase and under the marble console there lurked an ominous shadow. She did not want to run away but her heart seemed to turn over.

Her old jacket was hanging over the back of a chair. Anna had probably cleaned it with benzine, or else she had just taken it out of moth balls and put it there to air; it was very old and it looked very worn. It was old and worn but it could not complain as Françoise complained when she was hurt; it had no soul, it could not say to itself, "I'm an old worn jacket." It was strange; Françoise tried to imagine what it would be like if she were unable to say, "I'm Françoise, I'm six years old, and I'm in Grandma's house." Supposing she could say absolutely nothing: she closed her eyes. It was as if she did not exist; and yet other people would be coming here and see her and would talk about her. She opened her eyes again; she could see the jacket; it existed; yet it was not aware of itself. There was something disturbing, a little frightening in all of this. What was the use of its existing, if it couldn't be aware of its existence? She thought it over; perhaps there was a way. "Since I can say 'I,' what would happen if I said it for the jacket?" It was very disappointing; she could look at the jacket, see absolutely nothing but the jacket, and say very quickly, "I'm old, I'm worn"; but nothing happened. The jacket stayed there, indifferent, a complete stranger, and she was still Françoise. Besides, if she became the jacket, then she, Françoise, would never know it. Everything began spinning in her head as it did when she had a fit of anger and found herself, exhausted from crying and shouting, sprawled out on the floor. She went into her mother's room, took the book she had come for, and ran downstairs and out into the garden.

"L'Enfance de Françoise Miquel" [1]

She felt a sudden anguish; it was not a definite pain, but she began to delve deep into the past to unearth a similar pain. Then she remembered. The house was empty, the blinds had been drawn to shut out the sun, and it was dark; on the first-floor landing a little girl was standing flat against the wall, holding her breath. It was funny to be there all alone when everyone else was in the garden, it was funny and frightening; the furniture looked just as it always did, but at the same time it was completely changed: thick and heavy and secret; under the bookcase and under the marble console there lurked an ominous shadow. She did not want to run away but her heart seemed to turn over.

Her old jacket was hanging over the back of a chair. Anna had probably cleaned it with benzine, or else she had just taken it out of moth balls and put it there to air; it was very old and it looked very worn. It was old and worn but it could not complain as Françoise complained when she was hurt; it could not say to itself, "I'm an old worn jacket." It was strange; Françoise tried to imagine what it might be like if she were unable to say, "I'm Françoise, I'm six years old, and I'm in Grandma's house." Supposing she could say absolutely nothing: she closed her eyes. It was as if she did not exist at all; and yet other people would be coming here and see her and would talk about her. She opened her eyes again; she could see the jacket; it existed; yet it was not aware of itself. There was something disturbing, a little frightening, in all of this. What was the use of its existing, if it couldn't be aware of its existence? She thought it over; perhaps there was a way. "Since I can say 'I,' what would happen if I said it for the jacket?" It was very disappointing; she could look at the jacket, see absolutely nothing but the jacket, and say very quickly, "I'm old, I'm worn"; but nothing happened. The jacket stayed there, indifferent, a complete stranger, and she was still Françoise. Besides, if she became the jacket, then she, Françoise would never know it. Everything began spinning in her head and she ran downstairs and out into the garden.

She Came to Stay [2]

I have related elsewhere how, at Meyrignac, I stupidly gazed at an old jacket thrown over the back of a chair. I tried to put myself, as it were, inside the jacket, and say: "I am a tired old jacket." It was quite impossible, and I was panic-stricken. In the darkness of the past, in the stillness of inanimate beings I had dire forebodings of my own extinction; I conjured up delusive fallacies, and turned them into omens of the truth, and of my own death.

Memoirs of a Dutiful Daughter [3]

This is the incident that, with variations, appears most frequently in the writing of Simone de Beauvoir. Its importance is enhanced because it opens one of her earliest works, the unpublished *récit* of the childhood of Françoise Miquel. The incident tells of a child's initial intuition of nothingness and death. It marks the first discovery of the self and simultaneously of other people, of the solitude of the self and of its precariousness and mortality. It announces the poetic leitmotif of all the encounters with death, "Nothing will have taken place but the place." This is one of the main lines in Mallarmé's poem *Un Coup de dés*, which Simone de Beauvoir often quotes, in a truncated form, in the last volume of her memoirs.

Between the *récit* of the childhood of Françoise Miquel and *L'Invitée* the incident underwent very few changes, but they are significant. In the *récit* we begin with the incident, whereas in *L'Invitée* we get to it through memory. In the *récit*, near the beginning and towards the end of the passage, there are two long sentences that have been omitted in *L'Invitée:* "the stairs . . . had creaked . . ."; "when she had a fit of anger." These omissions contain information that is not essential to the anecdote. In the first the details given tell about the silence of the room and the domain of the doors, one of which Françoise will open at the end of the passage. The second sentence explains the first. In *L'Invitée* the passage begins with a flashback; in the *récit* it ends with a flashback that takes us still further into past time. The confusion the child feels she has already felt in a more amorphous and primitive state. This emphasizes the primeval quality of the incident. The reason why the child is alone in the house—the book which she came to get, undoubtedly for her mother—could be expanded into a symbol of the salvation to which she will eventually turn. The incident in the *récit*, a bit longer, a bit rougher, more explicit, has passed almost unchanged into *L'Invitée*. The quotation from the *Mémoires d'une jeune fille rangée* contains an incisive statement of what this incident means.

The experience is presented through a conventional psychological narrative structure. A present anguish recalls a past anguish: a feeling resurrects a scene, an important event. It is a moment of heightened awareness, indeed an epiphany which the child is unable to bear. She flees. The absence-presence of the jacket, the presence-absence of the self evoke the entire drama of consciousness and of death, the very quality of human contact with reality. The movement of the scene from anguish to flight is the pattern which almost all the encounters follow.

The anguish, the climate in which the experience originally took place and is recalled, is never overcome. It is evaded and, it would seem, eventually disappears. It can be evoked by a memory which tends to separate the incident from everyday life and experience. This anguish, then, is an anomaly. It comes to the fore only on special occasions, when Françoise is alone, withdrawn from the others, who are together.

The place that is evoked in the recollection is a grandmother's house, an empty, dark house. Empty of people, not things. The child stands on the first-floor landing, alone. The others are in the garden, in the sun. This is the child's first experience with being alone, separate from the family community. Her stance, when we first see her: "a little girl was standing flat against the wall, holding her breath," tells us that something unusual, something fearful has happened, is happening. The child's point of view is maintained by the word "funny," which underlines the bizarreness, the newness of the experience. This is the first time. It is "funny" to be alone, but more important still "it was frightening." "Anguish," "pain" (*souffrance*), and "pain" (*malaise*) preceded "frightening," which is the more specific of the terms. The key to the passage is in the word "alone." Because she is alone she feels funny and afraid; therefore, she sees a familiar decor, familiar objects for the first time. Their transformation is not in their appearance. The furniture is recognizable, the bookcase and the marble console, solid bourgeois objects, are what they have always been. But the effect they produce is radically different, or rather they produce an effect by themselves for the first time. They, too, stand alone, separate. The three adjectives used to describe them: "thick," "heavy," "secret," suggest a living immobility, a mysterious and weighty presence. The verb "lurked," in the imperfect in French, reinforces the motionless and sluggish quality of the scene, the tomblike atmosphere, in short the intimation of death.

The effect produced tells us by analogy what the child feels. It is difficult to sort out the physical from the psychological-metaphysical; any analysis must refer to all these domains. The child has trouble breathing; "holding her breath" and "her heart seemed to turn over" indicate that she is not breathing normally; she is breathing the way we breathe under conditions of stress, in moments of anxiety. This abnormal breathing can in turn react on other physiological processes, transforming our physical presence in the world from something unconscious to something of which we are uncomfortably aware. The child is heavy, oppressed, and if she has no desire to "run away" it is because she, too, is stagnating. She is dying. Away from the family circle she has no identity. She is like a bookcase or a marble console, a piece of furniture: present but anonymous. There is no one to look at her; she is aware of herself as she has never been before.

With the introduction of the "old jacket" the anguish augments and the analysis becomes more precise. The jacket is "old and worn," a definite progression in feeling from "thick," "heavy," "secret." The jacket's situation, its hanging on the back of a chair, is at first explained away. The maid Anna (is she, too, perhaps, old and tired?) has left it there to air, either because she cleaned it or because she took it out of storage. In any case there is the suggestion of an unpleasant odor and the need for fresh air. But the situation never can, never does explain away the condition. Whatever is said about the jacket it remains old and worn. These anthropomorphic adjectives propose an absolute definition. At the same time they confer human qualities on the jacket. If a person is old and worn a person feels old and worn. Feeling should be followed by some verbalization of what it is one feels. It is precisely when feelings are unpleasant, negative, that we speak or write. Françoise, although she is only six, has already had recourse to words in times of personal difficulty. The comparison between Françoise, the child, and the jacket is made immediately. The only significant difference between them is that Françoise can and the jacket cannot speak. Not to be able to "say" (and "to say" is the second key word of the passage), is to lose one's hold on the known world.

Françoise's reaction to this confrontation with the jacket builds up in the same way, although it will go much further, as in her confrontation with the empty house. "It was funny," she thought earlier. "It was strange," she thinks now. The difference between the two massive pieces of furniture and the old, limp jacket underlines the difference in the effect they produce on the child. The furniture is always there. The jacket has a more complicated existence. It is put away in a closet, it is let out to air, it is worn by someone. By whom? Whose jacket is it? The furniture stands or sits by itself, self-contained, whereas the jacket is always on a hanger, or a person, or a chair. It is dependent on another object or being; it cannot stand or sit alone. The difference in texture between the furniture and the jacket becomes a psychological difference and indicates the child's progressive physical weariness.

It is obvious why the child's anguish would crystallize around the jacket, why it is the jacket that would prompt the important effort to imagine. The verb "to imagine" is Françoise's first attempt to go beyond her known world, to conceive of other modes of perceiving and being. Françoise's first act of consciousness is an act of negation. She tries to imagine what it would be like to be an old jacket, or rather what it would be like not to be Françoise. She envisages being and nothingness exclusively in terms of language. The data she gives us as a definition of her being is simple: her name, her age, her situation, spatial and tribal. She has the courage to go beyond the possibility of not being Françoise to the more appalling possibility of not being at all. She closes her eyes for greater concentration in order not to be taken in by habitual processes of perception. Not seeing is like not being. The other people, and it is interesting that she does not specify members of the family (she has temporarily moved beyond her particular world to a more abstract meditation), would react to her as she reacts to the jacket; they would "come," "see," and most important "speak." She would be, like the jacket, an unconscious object; that is to say—but Françoise neither says it nor as yet comprehends it—dead. When Françoise opens her eyes nothing in the decor around her has changed, but Françoise has made a leap forward in awareness. The jacket exists and doesn't know it. The participles "disturbing" and "frightening" are echoes of "funny," "strange," and "was frightening." The strangeness and fear continue; it is not even suggested that they have augmented; they seem far from being, or becoming, unbearable.

With the first interrogative sentence the tempo of the meditation changes. Françoise makes one last effort to give consciousness to the jacket, to speak for the jacket. The defeat of language

is total; there are no magic words. The jacket remains "indifferent," a "stranger," and Françoise, the would-be creator, remains
Françoise. The gulf between the subject and the object, the I
and the world, is unbridgeable. The last revelation, introduced
by "Besides," is the most important and the one that finally breaks
the child. Françoise understands what it would mean if she herself were absent. It would mean being like the old, tired jacket.
The revelation of her own death interrupts the meditation and
makes any further attempt at coping with the problem impossible. We are not even told how she feels. We know only of the
confusion in her head and her flight, her escape to the known
world of the family in the garden.

The confrontation with the absurd, which is always, whatever
its form, an anguished encounter with death, is followed by a
return to the human community. The return is made in order to
forget, in order to seek comfort. It is not a return made with a
new insight that could be incorporated into a new synthesis. In
all of Simone de Beauvoir's writings the empty house with the
solitary, anguished human presence remains isolated from "the
others" in their sunlit garden. They are imagined to be as full
as the child is empty. There is during this entire scene an implicit
hostility to the others, who are not suffering, who are different.
The encounter with nothingness is always felt subjectively. There
is rarely any sense of the mortality, of the potential for suffering
of the others; that they do indeed suffer is always a surprise.
Simone de Beauvoir's naïveté has its source in a supreme and
limiting egoism.

Language is the only means that Françoise possesses of holding
on to her world or of attempting to come to terms with new and
strange experiences. Françoise has nothing of the mystic. She is
already, at the age of six, an antimystic, as her model and creator,
Simone de Beauvoir, is to this day. The aim of the mystical experience is the breaking down of the ego, the individual personality, in order to perceive the world beyond the limits of our
physical and psychological conditioning. Mysticism presupposes

the existence of a force or forces with which we can enter into communion if certain barriers are removed. Its goal is not lucidity but ecstasy.

Françoise's first encounter with death and nothingness, her first metaphysical experience, establishes the pattern that is continued by all the characters in Simone de Beauvoir's works who undergo similar experiences. The ego discovers itself as unique, fragile, mortal, and is terrified of losing itself. These are classical anxiety symptoms, but they should not be dismissed merely as signs of a neurotic personality. On the contrary they are essential to any real comprehension of being. A purely psychological explanation of the child's anguish, her hostility at not being with her family for example, would provide only minimal and superficial answers. Solitude is not a sickness; it is a fact, the most difficult, perhaps, to accept.

In Simone de Beauvoir's world, language is the only instrument, and it is always an ineffective one, by which the human being attempts to hold on to his ego and understand the mystery without abdicating reason. This rigorous antimysticism would be admirable if it were not accompanied by another form of evasion. The mystic leaps beyond death in order to look down on it and eventually to welcome it. Simone de Beauvoir's characters leap to other people, to worldly commitment, as if death and the anguish it provokes did not exist.

This scene describes an essential discovery concerning *the* fact of the human condition and an early refusal to assimilate this discovery into the fabric of everyday life. Instead of being always present it is relegated to the domain of recurrent bouts of anguish, occasional awareness of the human condition. The anguish of an awareness of death is reserved for special occasions. Since she dwells on it only during extraordinary moments, death becomes unreal, the exception rather than the rule.

This short scene is powerful because of the child's point of view:

In particular, it often happens that children who are not yet anchored in their little corner of the universe, feel the shock of their "being in the world" as they feel their bodies. For example, the discovery of the self described by Lewis Carroll in *Alice in Wonderland* and by Richard Hughes in *High Wind in Jamaica* is a metaphysical experience; the child discovers in a concrete manner his presence in the world, his helplessness, his freedom, the opaqueness of things, the antagonism of other conscious beings.[4]

It might be suggested that this kind of experience is more likely to occur when the child is in some degree alienated both from the structures imposed by the family and from those imposed by organized religion. It might be suggested, too, that the child who has undergone this kind of metaphysical initiation will never be quite as docile as the child who has not, and that this experience, if it does indeed take place, will be the central experience of the entire life.

In the life of the fictional character Françoise Miquel, as well as in the life of Simone de Beauvoir, this scene retains its power precisely because it was a childhood experience of sufficient importance to be recalled voluntarily and involuntarily. It plays a role in the world of Simone de Beauvoir similar to the role played by the good-night kiss in Proust's novel *A la recherche du temps perdu*. It is present even when it is absent, as a necessary foundation—psychological and metaphysical—for the structures and images that come later. It tells us, in advance, where the weakness of characters and author lie. It represents, in both cases, the crucial drama and the essential evasion.

CHAPTER III

The Death of God

That was my first disappointment concerning religion and priests, and I never really fully recovered. I had for so long confused God and the Abbé Mirande that I began to wonder whether God was not also on the side of my mother, of the finicky old cranks who ran the Institute Joliet, of the books designated for young people in the catalogue of the Family Library; but this God was so nonsensical that I soon doubted his existence. The first time that this doubt took hold of me, I was very frightened. I was in the country lying on a bed of moss; the top of a birch tree was swaying above my head. I wasn't thinking about anything, but in the middle of an immense silence, it seemed as if the world had suddenly been emptied out. No one ordered the trees, the sky, the grass to exist and I was floating gratuitously among those vague appearances of nothingness; I jumped to my feet. I couldn't bear the anguish; I ran towards the house, to human voices. It's a funny feeling, after having lived in a world peopled by angels and saints under the gaze of an all powerful being, to find one-self suddenly alone among blind things.

"Marguerite," in "La Primauté du spirituel" [1]

No, I shan't meet death today. Not today or any other day. I'll be dead for others and yet I'll never have known death.

I closed my eyes again, but I couldn't sleep. Why had death entered my dreams once more? It is prowling inside me; I can feel it prowling there. Why?

I hadn't always been aware that one day I would die. As a

child, I believed in God. A white robe and two shimmering wings were awaiting me in heaven's vestry and I wanted so much to break through the clouds and try them on. I would often lie down on my quilt, my hands clasped, and abandon myself to the delights of the hereafter. Sometimes in my sleep I would say to myself, "I'm dead," and the voice watching over me guaranteed me eternity. I was horrified when I first discovered the silence of death. A mermaid had died on a deserted beach. She had renounced her immortal soul for the love of a young man and all that remained of her was a bit of white foam without memory and without voice. "It's only a fairy tale," I would say to myself for reassurance.

But it wasn't a fairy tale. *I* was the mermaid. God became an abstract idea in the depths of the sky, and one evening I blotted it out altogether. I've never felt sorry about losing God, for He had robbed me of the earth. But one day I came to realize that in renouncing Him I had condemned myself to death. I was fifteen, and I cried out in fear in the empty house. When I regained my senses, I asked myself, "What do other people do? What will I do? Will I always live with this fear inside me?"

From the moment I fell in love with Robert, I never again felt fear, of anything.

The Mandarins [2]

I regarded life as a happy adventure; my faith protected me from the terrors of death: I would close my eyes when my time came, and in a flash the snowy hands of angels would transport me to the celestial regions. . . . time and again I would lie down on the carpet, close my eyes, and join my hands in prayer, and then command my soul to make its escape. It was only a game; if I had really believed my final hour had come, I should have shrieked with terror. But the idea of death at least did not frighten me. One evening, however, I was chilled to the marrow by the idea of personal extinction. I was reading about a mermaid who was dying by the sad sea waves; for the love of a handsome prince, she had renounced her immortal soul, and was being changed into sea-foam. That inner voice which had always told her "Here I am" had been silenced forever, and it seemed to me that the entire universe had foundered in the ensuing stillness. But—no, it couldn't be. God had given me the promise of eternity: I could not ever cease to see, to hear, to talk to myself. There *could* be no end. . . .

I used to lose myself completely in these dizzy and futile speculations, and vainly refuse to admit the unbridgeable gap between consciousness and time.

Memoirs of a Dutiful Daughter [3]

Yet the face of the universe changed. More than once during the days that followed, sitting under the copper beech or the silvery poplars I felt with anguish the emptiness of heaven. Until then, I had stood at the center of a living tableau whose colors and lighting God Himself had chosen; all things murmured softly of His glory. Suddenly everything fell silent. And what a silence! The earth was rolling through space that was unseen by any eye, and, lost on its immense surface, I stood, alone, in the midst of sightless regions of the air. Alone: for the first time I understood the terrible significance of that word. Alone: without a witness, without anyone to speak to, without refuge. The breath in my body, the blood in my veins, and all this hurly-burly in my head existed for no one. I got up and ran back to the garden and sat down under the catalpa between Mama and Aunt Marguerite, so great was my need to hear a human voice.

I made another discovery. One afternoon, in Paris, I realized that I was condemned to death. I was alone in the house and I did not attempt to control my despair; I screamed and tore at the red carpet. And when, dazed, I got to my feet again, I asked myself: "How do other people manage? How shall *I* manage to . . ." It seemed to me impossible that I could live all through life with such horror gnawing at my heart. When the reckoning comes, I thought, when you're thirty or forty and you think "It'll be tomorrow," how on earth can you bear the thought? Even more than death itself I feared that terror which would soon be with me always.

Fortunately, in the course of the school year these metaphysical fulgurations were rare: I hadn't enough free time and solitude. My changed attitude did not affect my daily life. I had stopped believing in God when I discovered that God had no influence on my behavior: so this did not change in any way when I gave Him up. I had always imagined that the logical necessity of moral laws depended on Him: but they were so deeply engraved on my spirit that they remained unaltered for me after I had abolished Him.

Memoirs of a Dutiful Daughter [4]

God dies for Simone de Beauvoir and for her major female characters when they are about fifteen years old. What God? The God whose image Simone de Beauvoir had interiorized as a child tells us more about the Catholic bourgeoisie by which she was conditioned than about any serious theological investigation. Indeed the whole theogony she describes, with the snowy bands of angels and the starry heavens, suggests the glossy prints in cheap Bibles, the Catholicism without pain of those who believe by habit or convenience and who seek in religion social and moral respectability and comfort. It is Catholicism without metaphysics or mysticism. The death of the God who rules this saccharine heaven hardly seems to carry the ominous weight of Nietzsche's famous cry, "God is dead." Nonetheless, Simone de Beauvoir's God was a god, and whatever one may think about the tinselled decor that surrounded him, he did give, as gods do, order and structure to the world. As long as he was, a great number of questions could never be asked. His presence assured the planet and the persons on it of a stability and a justification without which most human beings are incapable of functioning. When God dies in these texts it is an abstract death, rather like that of a very distant relative. The consequences and implications of his death are not always immediately felt. When they are, then the death of God precipitates the reign of death.

Here again the earliest text contains all the facts, themes, and patterns of this particular encounter with death. God begins to die because of the intrusions of a gossipy, moralizing priest. The association of the priest and God in the child's mind is understandable. God is envisaged in relatively simple terms as a male, authoritarian figure who has absolute, unquestionable knowledge concerning good and evil. It is to the priest-God that confessions are made and from him that absolution is received. Nothing in the human or natural world seriously contradicts the domination of this figure. Indeed the natural world speaks of God's presence. When contradictions arise they have their source in the behavior of the Godhead. The silliness of the priest weighs more heavily than the metaphysical-moral universe he upholds. Once the priest is felt to be similar in kind to the frivolous, narrow-minded, and inferior Catholic women in the child's entourage, then God, like Humpty Dumpty, is precariously perched and ready to fall.

The first intimations of God as a fictional character are calmly contemplated; those that follow are suffused with anguish. The decor is almost always the same: the country, nature, once God's undisputed domain, and the child-adolescent, alone and silent. Silence, as in the encounter with the old jacket, is the essential factor. There is no anguish without silence; there is no encounter and no revelation. Silence is not only the absence of noise in the outer world; it is the absence of inner noises—thoughts, or more modestly notions and images whirling around in the head: "I wasn't thinking about anything." The physical situation of the child "lying on a bed of moss" plays an important role in creating this inner silence, as if physical immobility and a limited visual perspective—"the top of a birch tree was swaying above my head"—prevented the mind from wandering in its usual manner and forced upon it a confrontation in concentration that it would normally shun. What happens, happens suddenly. This is the particular rhythm of all revelations. Again as in the encounter with the old jacket it is the familiar decor that changes first, that becomes actively present. Then the child lives her own absence. The verb "to become empty," stronger here than would have been the substantive or the adjective "empty," emphasizes the abrupt and overwhelming feeling of confusion and falling away. The particular situation becomes a microcosm of the cosmos suddenly deprived of the laws of gravity, where trees, the sky, the grass, and the child herself float aimlessly in space, detached from any of the objective or subjective structures that habitually keep things in their acceptable places. The resemblances between this description and clinical descriptions of anxiety attacks, as we have already noted in the confrontation with the old jacket, cannot be overlooked. The symptoms are disturbingly similar. These are anxiety attacks whose origins are purportedly metaphysical. The child, according to Simone de Beauvoir, is undergoing a metaphysical crisis. Whether one can, in fact, experience a metaphysical crisis that is not dependent on some deep psychic turmoil is a question that psychoanalysts would probably raise. Simone de Beauvoir never suggests that the unconscious is in any manner responsible for these attacks. She is opposed to explanations that limit the moral responsibility and the intellectual control of the human being.

The child's reaction is the same here as in the encounter with the old jacket. She runs back to the others. In this episode it is to the house rather than the sunlit garden; it is where she is not and where the family is. Where she is is chaos; where they are is law and order. What is most striking at the end of this scene is the specific value given to "human voices," which are opposed to the silence that informed the revelation. Voices are more than noise. They are words; they give explanations and justifications, they distract. Voices reassure. They tell stories about the world; they are the antithesis of chaos. Voices replace the fallen God. In the silence that follows the disappearance of the heavenly cohorts, the bustling world of angels and saints, is the word—without God.

The other texts contain variations on this earlier one. The revelation is always followed by a flight; the encounter is always presented as an essential moment in the past life of the character, a moment of truth that it is impossible to go beyond, to explore further, a truth to be avoided. The revelations expose Simone de Beauvoir's irremediable "bad faith."

The second text, from *Les Mandarins*, elaborates on the earlier text and corroborates it. Anne, the central figure in the novel, is plagued from the beginning to the end of the book by the presence of death, her own and that of others, in war and in peace. She is plagued, too, by the imminence of old age. Within the group of mandarins busily acting and trying to act on the world in a particular place at a particular time Anne, the only character who says "I," pursues a confused meditation on death and love.

Love is a fete that can become a temporary bulwark against the obsession of death. But love dies, too, fades away to be more exact, and the only reality is death. "Vanity of vanities; all is vanity" is the leitmotif of Anne's monologue.

Anne, like the major figures in the other texts, is alone. She is in her bed for the duration of her first monologue and the bed— a place to be born, a place to sleep and dream, a place to love and to die—accentuates her despair. In everyday life the bed is essentially a place to sleep. Because she is not sleeping—the result of too much alcohol at the party to celebrate the end of World War II that opens the novel—her agitation is increased. Unusual physiological conditions often precede acute psychological and metaphysical experiences. They lower the defenses created by habit and routine and allow hidden monsters to rush in. Many of Simone de Beauvoir's characters often overindulge.

The opening paragraphs of the monologue, our initial contact with Anne's first-person voice, disclose the central drama of the novel which is resolved, unsatisfactorily as always, in Anne's last monologue more than five hundred pages later. Death is a fact: she knows it will come to her; she sees it come to others. In *Les Mandarins* the most unacceptable death is that of Diego, Nadine's young poet-lover, during the occupation. Yet death is elusive. It is what we know most and least. Dying we can and shall know, but the state of being dead we shall never know. Anne's central obsession is the fear of being dead, of nothingness. Fear, too, of those moments when the anguish of the reality of death over-whelms her and leads her to attempt escape through love, work, political activity, all *divertissements* that fail. The *divertissements* always involve other people. The anguish is born and nurtured in solitude; it is temporarily exorcised by some form of contact with other human beings. "The others" in this context are a haven.

The verb "to prowl" in the second paragraph captures the in-sinuating, pervasive presence of death and its evil intentions. Anne's question, which seems naïve, concerns the origin of this sudden preoccupation with death. The return to the past serves a double function. It develops the notion that there are periods of one's life with and periods of one's life without anguish. It suggests the reason why this anguish should suddenly reappear. The idea of God masks the reality of death. Because she believed in God Anne did not know that she would die, was indeed dying. God, for the child, meant an eternal paradise which she eagerly sought. The position in which she placed herself for the great moment of entrance into paradise—"I would often lie down on my quilt, my hands clasped"—is the same position, without "my hands clasped," in which she will find herself during most of her moments of anguish. The center of opposition in this scene is once again between "the voice" and "the silence." To be able to say "I'm dead" annihilates nothingness and confirms the doctrine of eternal personal immortality. The "delights" are abruptly transformed into horror. The transition is made through a fairy tale which reiterates the Mallarmean "nothing will have taken place but the place." What is important is neither the love story nor the fact that the "mermaid" becomes "a bit of white foam" but that she is "without memory and without voice." What then becomes of her love for the young man? It is as if it had never been; to be immortal is to be able to use words, to tell the story of one's life.

Between the statements that it was only a fairy tale and that it wasn't a fairy tale, the essential conversion takes place. Anne becomes partially the "mermaid" condemned to be "without memory and without voice," which is another, more concrete way of saying, condemned to death. The anguish becomes a reality through the mediation of the fairy tale, which proposes a concrete image: the mermaid, the love story, the white foam. The anguish is not the result of logical, philosophical deductions based on the consequences of the death of God. Moreover Simone de Beauvoir's protagonists do not kill God-the-thief. They erase him, wipe him away as if he were a word on a blackboard; he suffers the same fate as the mermaid in the fairy tale and the "ladies of yesteryear" in Villon's famous ballad. The disappearance is total; they leave no visible trace. But their absence is a gaping hole that can never be filled. The day that Anne understands that she is condemned to death, that she is aware of the hole, there are no words: "I cried out in fear in the empty house." Again the solitude, again a reaction that suggests an adolescent anxiety attack. The question she asks herself after she recovers is, How can one live with the intimate knowledge of death? For the first time the anguish is related to all humanity. But the death of others is, for Simone de Beauvoir's protagonists, a significantly abstract notion. Their anguish is egocentric; it can never be a stepping-stone to solidarity or knowledge. "From the moment I fell in love with Robert, I never again felt fear, of anything." Anne's leap, like that of the anguished child, is to other people in this case, a new god, a new guarantee of law and order as well as a source of perpetual intellectual adventure. As the mermaid heroically gave up her immortal soul for the love of a young man, Anne Dubreuil and, along with her, Françoise in *L'Invitée* and Hélène in *Le Sang des autres* and Simone de Beauvoir in the memoirs abjectly surrender their "souls," that is to say their awareness, to a superior man. At the end of this text we understand that if death is once again prowling it is because Anne's relations with Robert are no longer what they were. How she tries to avoid a real confrontation with death is a major part of the story of *Les Mandarins*. In the end she makes of her family —her daughter Nadine and her granddaughter Maria—a *raison d'être* less compelling than Robert but nonetheless efficient. The "bad faith" is total and unquestionable: "for me, [Sartre's] existence justified the world that for him nothing justified." [5] What Simone de Beauvoir is in fact saying is God is dead; long live Sartre.

The last two texts in which the death-of-God experience is related are in the *Mémoires d'une jeune fille rangée*, and they are a synthesis of elements in the two earlier texts: the anguish in the park, the anguish in the apartment; the words "alone" and "silence" and always the flight. One new ingredient helps us to substantiate the "bad faith." "Even more than death itself I feared that terror which would soon be with me always." The fear of a permanent anguish is in itself more horrendous than the fact of death. Deliberately to avoid this "terror" is to avoid further consideration of death. "These metaphysical fulgurations" is a verbal means of suppressing an essential intuition by suggesting that this kind of intuition is reserved for the privileged few, those who have "free time and solitude," in short, the despicable bourgeois.

So the anguish is temporarily resolved by the child who runs to the family in the garden or in the house, by the woman who runs to a man or to her child and grandchild or to an ideology that claims to explain the socioeconomic origin of the anguish. The movement is thus from an intense nonverbal experience to the comfort and logic of words. The word "God" is replaced by other less powerful words that are manipulated in such a way as to serve a similar function. The necessity of God is not dead in the world of Simone de Beauvoir. The characters leap towards a figure or a cause that will give them the same sense of security they knew with God as children. They leap towards the old harmony; the anguish is so strong that God never really dies.

Or rather, as the last sentence in the last quotation from the *Mémoires d'une jeune fille rangée* implies, a God who was once is always. There is no escape from the God of one's childhood.

CHAPTER IV

The Death of Others:
Initial Encounters

I knew a child who cried because his concierge's son was dead. His parents let him cry and then they became annoyed. "After all the little boy was not your brother." The child wiped his eyes. But it was a dangerous precept. Yes, it is useless to cry over a stranger. But why cry over one's brother?

Pyrrhus et Cinéas [1]

I was eight years old when for the first time I came face to face with the original evil. I was reading in the gallery; my mother came in with an expression on her face that we often noticed, an expression full of guilt and apology, and she said: "Louise's baby is dead."

Once again I see the twisted staircase, the stone corridor with those many doors, all alike; Mother told me that behind every door there was a room in which a whole family lived. We went in. Louise took me in her arms, her cheeks were flabby and wet; Mother sat on the bed beside her and began to talk to her in a low voice. In the cradle was a white-faced baby with closed eyes. I looked at the red tiles, at the bare walls, at the gas ring, and I began to cry. I was crying, Mother was talking, and the baby remained dead. In vain could I empty my money-box and Mother could sit up for nights together: it would always be just as dead.

"What's the matter with that child?" asked my father. "He went with me to see Louise," my mother answered. She had already told them the story, but now, with words, she tried to make them feel it: meningitis, the night of agony, and in the morning the little stiff body. Father listened as he swallowed his soup. I could not eat. Over there Louise was crying, she was not eating; nothing would ever give the child back to her—no, not ever. Nothing would blot out that unhappiness which fouled the world.

"Come now, drink your soup," said my father. "Everyone's finished."

"I'm not hungry."

"Do try a little, darling," said Mother.

I lifted the spoon to my lips and put it back on the plate with a kind of hiccup. "I can't!"

"Listen," said my father, "it's very sad that Louise's baby is dead, I'm deeply grieved for her, but not all our life are we going to mourn it. Now, just you hurry up!"

I drank. In a trice the hard voice had loosened the tightness about my throat. I felt the lukewarm liquid slip down my throat, and with each mouthful something flowed into me that was far more nauseating than the smell of the printing works. But the tightness was relieved. Not all our life.

Tonight, until the dawn and perhaps for a few more days—but not all our life—after all, it is her sorrow, not ours. It is her death. They had laid him on the bench with his torn collar and the blood caked on his face; his blood, not mine. "I'll never forget it." Marcel too cried in his heart. "Never, oh little one, my little pony, my good little boy—never will I forget your laughter and your living eyes." And his death is deep in our lives, peaceful and strange, and we who live remember; we live to remember it now that it no longer exists, any more than it existed for him who is dead. Not all our life—not even for a few days—not even for a minute. You are alone on that bed, and I can only hear the labored breath that comes from your lips, which you cannot hear.

He had drunk his soup and eaten all his dinner. Now he was crouching under the grand piano; the crystal chandelier shone with many fires; the crystallized fruits sparkled under their sugary casings; soft and tinted like sugar cakes, the lovely ladies smiled at each other. He looked at his mother: she did not look like those scented, fairylike beings; a black gown bared her shoulders; her hair, dark as her gown, was twisted smoothly round her head like a band of watered silk, but in her presence he did not think of flowers or splendid cakes, or of seashells, or of blue-tinted shingle on the beach. She was a human presence, no more. She

hurried from one end of the drawing-room to the other in her
tiny satin slippers, the heels of which were far too high, and she
smiled too—even she. A short time ago her face had been dis-
tressed, her low, intense voice had whispered in Louise's ear; now
she smiled. "Not all our life." He had dug his nails into the carpet.
Louise's baby is dead. He forced himself to visualize the scene:
Louise sitting on the edge of the bed, crying. He had stopped
crying and at this very moment he was even looking through the
motionless, transparent picture at the mauve, green, and pink
dresses, and desires once more rose within him—a desire to bite
those creamy arms, to thrust his face into that hair, to crumple
those light silks like a petal. Louise's baby is dead. In vain; it is
not my sorrow.

*It is not my death. I close my eyes, I remain motionless, but I
am remembering things about myself, and her death enters into
my life, but I do not enter into her death.*

I slipped out from under the piano, and in bed I cried myself
to sleep because of that thing which had poured into my throat
with the tepid soup—more bitter than the sense of guilt—my sin.
The sin of smiling while Louise was weeping, the sin of shedding
my own tears and not hers. The sin of being another being.

The Blood of Others [2]

I only once came in contact with real destitution. Louise and
her husband, the roofer, lived in a room in the Rue Madame, a
garret right at the top of the house; she had a baby and I went to
visit her with my mother. I had never set foot in a building of
this kind before. The dreary little landing on which there were a
dozen identical doors made my heart sink. Louise's tiny room
contained a brass bedstead, a cradle, and a table on which stood a
small oil stove; she slept, cooked, ate, and lived with her husband
and child between these four walls; all around the landing there
were families confined to stifling little holes like this; the com-
parative promiscuity in which I myself had to live and the
monotony of bourgeois life oppressed my spirits. But here I got a
glimpse of a universe in which the air you breathed smelled of
soot, in which no ray of light ever penetrated the filth and
squalor: existence here was a slow death. Not long after that,
Louise lost her baby. I cried for hours; it was the first time I had
known misfortune at first hand. I thought of Louise in her cheer-
less garret without her baby, without anything: such terrible dis-

tress should have shaken the world to its foundations. "It's not right!" I told myself. I wasn't only thinking of the dead child but also of that sixth-floor landing. But in the end I dried my tears without having called society in question.

Memoirs of a Dutiful Daughter [3]

My uncle Maurice, having existed entirely on fresh green salad for two or three years, had died of stomach cancer after the most hideous sufferings. My aunt and Madeleine had mourned him long and loud. But eventually they found consolation, and life at La Grillère became much gayer than it had been in the past.

Ibid. [4]

Grandpapa died at the end of the autumn, after lingering interminably; my mother shrouded herself in black crepe and had all my clothes dyed black. This funeral get-up did not improve my appearance; it set me apart, and I felt that it condemned me to an austere way of life that was beginning to weigh heavily upon my spirits.

Ibid. [5]

A few days later, for the first time in my life, I saw someone die: my uncle Gaston, suddenly carried off by an intestinal obstruction. His death throes lasted a whole night. Aunt Marguerite sat holding his hand and saying things which he couldn't understand. His children, my parents, my sister, and I were with him when he died. He gave the death rattle, and vomited up some blackish stuff. When he stopped breathing, his jaw sagged, and a scarf was tied round his head to keep it in place. My father was sobbing openly: I had never seen him weep before. The violence of my own despair surprised everyone, including myself. I was very fond of my uncle, and I cherished the memory of our early-morning hunting expeditions at Meyrignac; I was very fond of my cousin Jeanne and I couldn't bring myself to say: she's an orphan. But neither these regrets nor my compassion could explain the storm of grief that swept over me during the next two days: I couldn't bear to think of that despairing glance which my uncle had cast at his wife just before he died, and in which the irreparable was already an accomplished fact. "Irreparable"; "irremediable": these words were hammering in my brain till I thought my head would burst; and there was another answering them:

"inevitable." Perhaps one day I, too, would see that look in the eyes of a man whom I would have loved all my life. It was Jacques who brought me comfort.

Ibid.[6]

The next morning, there was a letter from Meyrignac; Grandpapa was seriously ill, and was not expected to live; I was very fond of him, but he was very old, his death seemed natural now, and I could feel no sadness about it. . . . On the Sunday, a wire brought the news of Grandfather's death; my past was certainly being destroyed. . . .

The whole family had gathered at Meyrignac; it was perhaps because of this great upheaval that I remained unmoved by the sight of Grandpapa's dead body, the house, and the garden. . . .

Now I was ready for something else; I was all expectancy, and in the violence of this feeling all regrets were swept away.

Ibid.[7]

A meditation on one's own death may alternately provoke indifference or anguish. It is possible to watch oneself die a little each day, and, with more or less lucidity, depending on the physiological and mental state, it is possible to observe almost all of the last act. But one can never see oneself dead. Others are dead; we see others dead.

A child's first experience of death is usually the death of older members of the family, people in the family entourage, domestic pets. The bourgeois child normally meets death for the first time indirectly; he is protected by the words and gestures of adults from the reality of death and dying. He is spared the agony, the helpless gestures, the struggling, pitiful noises that mark the difficult passage from life to death. Often he does not see the corpse. The death of an animal may pose the same problem of suffering, the same mystery of absence; an animal, however, can be and is often immediately replaced.

The first encounters with the death of others in the writings of Simone de Beauvoir are the death of the maid Louise's baby, the death of older members of the family and the death of Simone de Beauvoir's best friend, Elizabeth Mabille. Each of these is described in the *Mémoires d'une jeune fille rangée;* the first and third are also transposed into fiction.

The earliest of these incidents takes place before the death of God when Simone de Beauvoir was about twelve years old. The incident is used at the very beginning of *Pyrrhus et Cinéas* and towards the beginning of *Le Sang des autres.* Its value as overture is evident. The death of Louise's baby is an occasion to expose the metaphysical as well as the social "scandal"; it is an occasion to point at the universal human condition and an unjust class situation. Of all the deaths confronted and related it is the one that most lends itself to the elaboration of an ideological message.

In *Pyrrhus et Cinéas* the incident plays several roles. It establishes the tone of the essay, which is more affirmative than the ambiguous tone of Simone de Beauvoir's novels. The essays are not instruments of discovery but rather a means of asserting truths and beliefs. They tend to be either dogmatic or pedantically documented, to contain too many examples and insufficient analysis. *Pyrrhus et Cinéas*, a lyrical essay on the joys of commitment, begins with a death that is immediately transformed into a social-moral problem. The incident is reduced to a few essential elements: the difference between the bourgeois child who cries and the concierge's dead baby; the difference between the child who cries and his annoyed parents; the difference between the moral lesson drawn by the parents and the moral lesson drawn by Simone de Beauvoir. The anecdote functions essentially as a means of avoiding the explicit biblical quotation "Am I my brother's keeper?" while at the same time suggesting it to the reader. At the outset there is a significant evasion.

Death is also used here to disclose one of Simone de Beauvoir's most persistent concerns: the relation to another person and to a very specific kind of other person, someone from a different social class. The spontaneous reaction of the child who cries and the learned reaction of the child who dries his eyes implies that

our relation to other people is an indoctrinated, conditioned relation. It implies, too, that our natural reactions are good.

In *Le Sang des autres*, a novel written at the same time as
Pyrrhus et Cinéas, the same anecdote is further developed. It
occupies a privileged place at the beginning of the novel and contains in miniature the sense of the entire novel and its title. Again
the significant evasion occurs; society is the killer and death becomes a question of moral responsibility. A difficult question, but
one for which in specific contexts—the Resistance movement during the war in France, for example—specific answers ran be found.
The same is not true for death itself; if Louise and her baby had
been of the same class as the sensitive bourgeois child-narrator, the
problem could not be envisaged in social or moral terms. Death
would have had to be encountered directly.

The passage in *Le Sang des autres*, because of its length, is one
of the most revealing. An essential question is avoided and transformed into an important but nonetheless secondary preoccupation. The narrator, Jean, is sitting at the deathbed of a young
woman who had been his mistress and, after much indecision, had
decided to work in his Resistance unit. Her imminent death im-
pells him to resurrect his past life. The greater part of this passage
is a flashback to his initial encounter with death when he was
eight years old. In the first paragraph the oblique references to a
specific milieu are more important than the death of the baby.
They continue to be so throughout. The emphasis is on the contrast between "reading in the gallery," "an expression full of guilt
[remords] and apology"—the activities, behavior, place, and
symptoms of the bourgeoisie—and "the original evil [scandale],"
"Louise's baby is dead." The narrator's bias is immediately disclosed in "for the first time." He is shocked that one can arrive
at the age of eight—"reading in the gallery"—without any contact
with a reality other than the one provided by books and the
bourgeois home. His mother's face relates the impotent guilt of
the sensitive bourgeoise.

The second paragraph does not deal uniquely with death, as

one might expect it would, but with a description of a human misery that could be alleviated. The "twisted staircase," the "stone corridor," the "doors, all alike," the "red tiles," the "bare walls" and the "gas ring" accentuate the concrete differences between the places in which the bourgeoisie and its servants live. It is Louise who makes the only gesture of human warmth. The narrator's mother talks; condescension is suggested. The narrator looks and cries. He does not look at the dead child, although he sees it, nor does he speak of it at first as being dead. The dead object and the idea of death do not immediately coincide. And then, suddenly, we move from the level of social misfortune to an absolute condition: "it would always be just as dead." This is the real revelation. But just as the child will stop crying and eat his soup so he will transmute the absoluteness of death into a relative social and human phenomenon. Death will become an accident, therefore avoidable.

The evening meal is an occasion for presenting different bourgeois attitudes: the mother's faith in words to console Louise, to touch her husband; the father's brutal, insensitive realism; the useless hypersensitivity of the bourgeois child; his initial inability to swallow his soup. Of the four negations the first two are temporary. The child will eat and, a bit later perhaps, so will Louise. The second two are eternal. "Nothing" and "not ever" underline the definitive quality of death in a universe without God. The second "nothing" introduces a more ambiguous clause. "That unhappiness which fouled the world" is the "original evil" of the first paragraph. It is no longer clear whether it refers to death or to social misery, or as is more likely, to both. Death and injustice have been assimilated, and death, by this assimilation, has lost its sting.

The narrator's father states, in its simplest terms, the theme of the second and concluding part of the passage: "not all our life are we going to mourn it." What is involved in this statement, which in itself is a cliché, is the fickleness of the human mind that is so easily distracted; even, eventually, from the most obsessive thoughts. Life goes on because the mind wanders. Simone de Beauvoir, however, is interested in preparing another conclusion to this statement: the absolute separation between consciousnesses, the gulf between any "I" and other people, the essential human solitude and the moral problem it poses in the domain of action: the problem of responsibility.

The narrator's first abdication and the proof of his father's words are in the verb "I drank." The soup goes down because he is not dead, Louise's baby is dead. The passage that follows is a meditation in the present tense on all of Jean's dead. It is addressed to the dying woman. The key word is "alone" and the compelling question is not death but the existence of other people and the degree to which the narrator is responsible for their deaths.

The concluding paragraph describes the child's awareness of his abdication, his futile attempts to maintain an obsessive sorrow and his final epiphany. The bourgeois decor, an evening reception, again plays an important role: the "grand piano" and the "crystal chandelier," the "crystallized fruits" and the "lovely ladies" which are so alien to his sorrow, so frivolous in comparison to death, gradually assume, for him as for his smiling mother, an ascendency over his distress. They are sensual symbols of life. The child cries and tears at the rug not because Louise's baby is dead but because he can never really enter, or so he and his creator think, into this death. He cries because of his guilt. Death has, in fact, been evaded.

By presenting each death as a particular phenomenon due to specific causes: poverty, political action, the Resistance movement; by refusing to generalize—all men die—or to identify—the narrator never thinks of himself as mortal—Simone de Beauvoir has led her characters, her readers, and herself astray.

She practices the same evasive tactics when she uses the incident, for the third and last time, in the *Mémoires d'une jeune fille rangée*. The sordid decor in which Louise, her husband, and the baby live assumes even greater importance. Death has become an adjunct of poverty, as if only the damned of the earth, "les misérables," suffered and died. The key expressions are the same here as in the passage from *Le Sang des autres:* "I only once came in contact with real destitution"; "it was the first time I had known misfortune at first hand"; such "distress should have shaken the world to its foundations." This first encounter with the death of another human being is less an encounter with death than an encounter with "society," a human and therefore a remediable injustice. Is it because this other human being was the maid's baby, or is it rather that any first death would have been converted into a social and moral problem? Although guilt is difficult to bear, it is less difficult than an uncluttered view of death.

Louise's baby dies in the autobiographical, fictional, and non-fictional writings. The four deaths of older members of Simone de Beauvoir's family—her uncle Maurice, her maternal grandfather, her uncle Gaston and her paternal grandfather—are recorded solely in the *Mémoires d'une jeune fille rangée.* Simone de Beauvoir's age at each of these encounters is important, but not easy to ascertain. The obituaries are presented here in the order in which they appear in the *Mémoires d'une jeune fille rangée* and cover roughly the years 1924 to 1929, during which time Simone de Beauvoir was between sixteen and twenty-one years old. At least four years—and the death of God—have passed between the death of Louise's baby and the first of the recorded family deaths: the death of Uncle Maurice. There is a grim humor in the first sentence. If the humor disappears in the two that follow, a matter-of-fact tone is maintained that perpetuates the distance separating the dying man, the dead man, the mourning family, and the narrator. This death is less important in itself than for the effect it has on the survivors. There is the suggestion that the death of this authoritarian uncle was something of a boon. Similar comments can be made about the second family death, that of "Grandpapa." The "lingering interminably" echoes the "hideous sufferings" of Uncle Maurice. They remain, in both cases, abstract, separated from any real apprehension of suffering on the part of the narrator, who seems to be reporting what she has been told. Again the conclusion is unrelated to the death and important because of the effect it has on Simone de Beauvoir. Like the duc de Guermantes in Proust's novel she is annoyed by the intrusion of death—"a bore"—who obliges her to conform to certain rituals. Death cramps her style. This death is a pretext to talk about social and moral constraints.

The third death is a direct encounter with dying and the words "for the first time" tell us, as they did in the episode of Louise's baby, that the event is praticularly significant. Obviously to watch someone die is not the same as learning about someone's death. There is no substitute for this particular experience. And yet the pattern of events strangely resembles the pattern in the episode of the old jacket. Experience is limited by past experience. The same evasive tactics are used each time the anguish is too strong.

The scene is presented in a simple and expressive manner. The two main elements are the dying uncle's physical manifestations— what the narrator sees—and the reactions and anguish of those who surround the deathbed. The horror is augmented by the contrast between the manner of being of the dying and the manner of being of the living. The dying man is a thing. He is the seat of uncontrollable perturbations: "he couldn't understand"; "he gave the death rattle"; "he vomited"; "his jaw sagged."

Among those who witness and participate in this deathbed agony, three are specifically mentioned: Aunt Marguerite, the wife of the dying man; the narrator's father and the narrator herself. The attitudes and gestures of Aunt Marguerite are those of a loving and faithful wife who is losing her husband and her *raison d'être*. The narrator's father "was sobbing . . . : I had never seen him weep before." The "never seen" is as significant as the "for the first time" of the first sentence. Her father's mental agitation is almost as important in conditioning her own reactions as the dying man's symptoms. Her own reactions are, of course, what the scene is all about. They are, in part, a synthesis of those of Aunt Marguerite and her father. The narrator never identifies explicitly with the dying man; she identifies rather with Aunt Marguerite, the woman who loses "a man whom I would have loved" for a long time. What is most significant is that the violence of the narrator's despair, the "storm of grief that swept over me during the next two days," is related neither to what she saw during her uncle's agony, nor to her affection for her dead, absent uncle, but to the awesome power of certain words: "irreparable"; "irremediable"; "inevitable." The three words that "were hammering in my brain till I thought my head would burst" are much stronger than the hypothetical image projected at the end of the scene, in which the narrator replaces Aunt Marguerite at the deathbed of the man she loves. The words imply an understanding of death which nothing in the scene, after the description of the agony, substantiates.

The last sentence reveals once again the pattern of evasion and flight. It is no longer the family circle towards which the child runs, but a man towards whom the young woman turns. The refusal not to be consoled is a major weakness. Jacques, or rather the role he fulfills, will be replaced by Jean-Paul Sartre, whose power to console and distract will prove to be infinite.

The fourth and last of the early family deaths tells us something we suspected all along: "I was very fond of him, but he was very old, his death seemed natural now," and she felt "no sadness about it." Death and the dead person are less important in themselves than the reaction they arouse in the narrator. If she is moved then death is moving: an "original evil." If she is not moved then death is envisaged as natural, an inevitable biological process that leads to a noisy family reunion. The key words are she felt "no sadness about it. . . . I remained unmoved." The inability to confront an experience that does not directly touch the feelings is a psychological and an intellectual limitation. It involves, as well as an excessive egotism, a dangerously restricted perspective. Because there is no sense of human suffering there is no sense of solidarity, either with others or with one's own past. Death becomes an occasional, unannounced visitor, a capricious event rather than a constant presence. The encounters, brief and sporadic, sometimes provoke tremendous intensity of feeling. The intensity is quickly dissipated and death relegated to a minor role.

CHAPTER V

The Death of Anne-Zaza

Anne's death was a surprise. Before being taken to Uzerche her body was laid out in a mortuary chapel. Her face was sallow and skeletal; her long black hair rooted in the dead flesh was spread out over the pillow, brittle, dull, still alive.

Pascal pressed his hands against his eyelids; he didn't want to keep looking at the emaciated cadaver surrounded by tapers and autumn flowers. Nothing of Anne was left in these carnal remains; in order to reach Anne's essential truth he would have to look deep into his own heart.

"Anne," in "La Primauté du spirituel" [1]

Anne's death had revealed to [Chantal] the ugliness of the world. Her enthusiasm had abated; faced with the absurdity of fate she would adopt a lucid bitterness.

Ibid. [2]

"It's the only consolation we have," said Madame Vignon, "the thought that her death will not have been useless to the glory of God."

Ibid. [3]

. . . How present Anne was within these old walls! Her golden eyes, her heavy bluish hair, her autumnal face, how I would like to make her live again; it would take an entire book to show her as she really was, a being of flesh and fervor; the beautiful heroine, transparent and mysterious, with her innocent laughter and her passionate heart. Why continue to regret the woman she would have become? Chantal had a mission to fulfill in behalf of the pathetic young girl whose image haunted the old living room. In the serene darkness of the old house she had at last met what she had been seeking for so long a time; something that belonged only to her and that others could envy. A beautiful and tragic story would forever weigh on her life; from now on mysterious shadows would sometimes pass over her face; her gestures, her words would have subtle echoes and people would gaze at her for a long time, anxious to penetrate her secret. Chantal bowed her head still further; this magnificent burden was heavy on her heart; she could not yet foresee all the riches it would bestow on her, but she already felt transformed by its presence; she would know better than before how to love, understand, illuminate, console; perhaps one day she would even be capable of transforming her unhappy experience into a work of quiet beauty.

"Anne darling, I shall never forget you," Chantal promised fervently.

Ibid.[4]

During the next four days in the clinic at Saint-Cloud she kept calling out for "my violin, Pradelle, Simone, champagne." The fever did not abate. Her mother had the right to spend the final night with her. Zaza recognized her and knew then that she was going to die. "Don't cry for me, Mama darling," she said. "There are outcasts in all families; I'm the outcast in ours."

When next I saw her, in the chapel at the clinic, she was laid on a bier surrounded by candles and flowers. She was wearing a long nightdress of rough cloth. Her hair had grown and now hung stiffly around a yellowed face that was so thin I hardly recognized her. The hands with their long, pale fingernails were folded on a crucifix, and seemed as fragile as an ancient mummy's. Madame Mabille was sobbing. "We have only been instruments in God's hands," Monsieur Mabille told her.

The doctors called it meningitis or encephalitis; no one was quite sure. Had it been a contagious disease, or an accident? Or had Zaza succumbed to exhaustion and anxiety? She has often appeared to me at night, her face all yellow under a pink sunbonnet, and seeming to gaze reproachfully at me. We had fought together against the revolting fate that had lain ahead of us, and for a long time I believed that I had paid for my own freedom with her death.

Memoirs of a Dutiful Daughter [5]

The most profound and the most moving encounter with death in the three volumes of Simone de Beauvoir's memoirs is the death of Zaza, whose real name was Elizabeth Mabille. This death is the most important of the early autobiographical encounters with death because of the intense relationship between Simone de Beauvoir and her friend.

Simone de Beauvoir wrote the first volume of her memoirs with the avowed intention of paying a debt to her childhood friend, who died perhaps of meningitis and surely of a broken heart at the moment when Simone de Beauvoir had successfully gained that freedom for which they had both, in different ways, been struggling. To describe the death of Zaza was, for many years, beginning in 1932, the goal of Simone de Beauvoir's creative activity. The attempt at the fictional transposition of this death, as we can see from the extract in "La Primauté du spirituel," was not successful. It was only in the *Mémoires d'une jeune fille rangée*, where she dropped the pretense of fiction, that she succeeded.

Until she met Zaza at school when she was nine years old, Simone de Beauvoir thought of herself as the "unique one," the almost perfect center of an almost perfect world. The dominant experience of Simone de Beauvoir's childhood, even stronger perhaps than her disenchantment with Catholicism and her parents, the death of God and the gods, was her passionate friendship for Zaza, a friendship which has been compared to that of Michel de Montaigne for Etienne de La Boétie [6] and which might also be compared to that of Saint Augustine, recorded in his *Confessions*, for a friend who died at an early age.

Zaza forms a contrast to Simone de Beauvoir's own image of herself as a dutiful daughter. Zaza never lost her mystical faith, nor did she reject the emotional and social demands of her family. But Zaza was a nonconformist whose exuberance, sensitivity, and originality dazzled her conventional friend. In the late childhood and early adolescence of Simone de Beauvoir, Zaza played a role somewhat analogous to that played by Swann and his daughter Gilberte in the life of Proust's narrator, or the role played by

Alain-Fournier's Grand Meaulnes in the life of François Seurel.
Zaza leads Simone de Beauvoir's emotions away from the confines
of the family circle; she encourages an expansion of her sensibility.

The pages that conclude the first of the four parts of the
Mémories d'une jeune fille rangée speak eloquently of this friend-
ship. Simone de Beauvoir is ten and a half and she has known
Zaza for a year.

I did not immediately consider what place this friendship had
in my life; I was still not much cleverer than I was as a baby at
realizing what was going on inside me. I had been brought up to
equate appearances with reality; I had not learned to examine
what was concealed behind conventions of speech and action. It
was taken for granted that I had the tenderest affection for all the
members of my family, including even my most distant cousins.
For my parents and sister I felt love, a word that covered everything. Nuances and fluctuations of feeling had no claim to
existence in my world. Zaza was my best friend: and that was
all. In a well-regulated human heart friendship occupies an honorable position, but it has neither the mysterious splendour of love
nor the sacred dignity of filial devotion. And I never called this
hierarchy of the emotions into question.

That year, as in all other years, the month of October brought
with it the exciting prospect of the return to school. The new
books cracked when I opened them, and smelled just as good;
seated in the leather armchair I gloated over what the future had
in store for me.

None of my expectations were realized. In the Luxembourg
Gardens there were the bonfire smells and the yellowing leaves of
autumn: they failed to move me; the blue of heaven had been
dimmed. The classes bored me; I learned my lessons and did my
homework joylessly, and pushed my way sullenly through the
front door of the Cours Désir. It was my own past coming to life
again, and yet I did not recognize it: it had lost all its radiant
colors; my life was dull and monotonous. I had everything, yet
my hands were empty. I was walking along the Boulevard Raspail
with Mama and I suddenly asked myself the anguished question:
"What is happening to me? Is this what my life is to be? Nothing
more? And will it always be like this, always?" The idea of living

through an infinity of days, weeks, months and years that were lighted by neither hope nor promise completely took my breath away: it was as if, without any warning, the whole world had died. But I was unable to give a name to this distress either.

For ten to fifteen days I dragged myself somehow, on legs that seemed as weak as water, from hour to hour, from day to day. One afternoon I was taking off my things in the cloakroom at school when Zaza came up to me. We began to talk, to relate various things that had happened to us, and to comment on them; my tongue was suddenly loosened, and a thousand bright suns began blazing in my breast; radiant with happiness, I told myself: "That's what was wrong; I needed Zaza!" So complete had been my ignorance of the workings of the heart that I hadn't thought of telling myself: "I miss her." I needed her presence to realize how much I needed her. This was a blinding revelation. All at once, conventions, routines, and the careful categorizing of emotions were swept away and I was overwhelmed by a flood of feeling that had no place in any code. I found myself moved by a wave of joy which went on mounting inside me, as violent and as fresh as a water fall, as naked, beautiful, and bare as a granite cliff. A few days later, arriving early at school, I looked in stupefaction at Zaza's empty seat. "What if she were never to sit there again, what if she were to die, then what would happen to me?" And again I was overcome by a revelation: "I can no longer live without her." It was rather frightening: She came and went unconcerned with my life and all my happiness, my very existence, lay in her hands. I imagined Mademoiselle Gontran coming in, her long black skirts sweeping the floor, and saying: "Children, let us pray; your little companion, Elizabeth Mabille, was called away to the arms of God last night." Well, if that were to happen, I told myself, I should die on the spot. I would slide off my seat and fall lifeless to the ground. This rationalization gave me comfort. I didn't really believe that God in his divine wisdom would take my life; neither did I really believe that I was afraid of Zaza dying. I had gone as far as to admit the extent of the dependence which my attachment to her placed upon me: I did not dare envisage all its consequences.

I didn't require Zaza to have any such definite feelings about me: it was enough to be her best friend. The admiration I felt for her did not diminish me in my own eyes. Love is not envy. I could think of nothing better in the world than being myself, and loving Zaza.[7]

The quality of tenderness in this passage is rare in the memoirs. It reappears in the pages that describe Zaza's illness and death and again, briefly, when Simone de Beauvoir speaks much later of the farewell kiss to Sartre, the soldier, in a crowded railway station, one of the few precise allusions to their physical intimacy. This emotional reticence gives an aesthetic dimension to these episodes which are more revealing than her lengthy enumerations and intellectual disquisitions. The dramatic moment in which she discovers the depth of her affection for Zaza contains in miniature the voyage described in the *Mémoires d'une jeune fille rangée*.

We are introduced to the child's state of mind as it reflects the moral and semantic universe of the family. She could not understand her true feelings for Zaza because the ready-made concepts of her entourage referred only to universal affections, not individual feelings, and so she had no words in her vocabulary which could describe them. "I had been brought up to equate appearances with reality." This, in Simone de Beauvoir's eyes, is the basic sin of her milieu. When she discovers the inadequacy of the closed, absolute order she had accepted as authority the young girl begins the struggle towards authenticity described in the *Mémoires d'une jeune fille rangée*.

Zaza's appearance in the cloakroom two weeks after the opening of school suddenly illumines and revives Simone de Beauvoir's dying world. It has all the attributes of a fete, a celebration. In a moment of almost mystical revelation, made more intense by the density of the imagery, the child realizes that the immediate cause of her depression was the absence of Zaza and that Zaza's presence is essential to her happiness. Her experience has broken through the conventions, routines, and clichés of her moral code. The reaction is one of boundless joy. A second revelation occurs a few days later when she looks at Zaza's vacant seat in the classroom and is struck by the possibility of Zaza's death. There is only one solution, an infantile evasion, here recognized as such, into "bad faith": her own imaginary death should Zaza die.

The scene ends on a note of triumph. The child has found the words that express her true feelings for Zaza; she has, as it were, invented on her own, an adequate conception of love.

There is a terrible irony in the events that follow: Zaza's death, here postulated as an improbable hypothesis, becomes a fact. The death of Zaza was not only the starting point for the *Mémoires d'une jeune fille rangée;* it also became with time the symbol of all of Simone de Beauvoir's formative years. Her revolt against church and family, her passionate hatred of the bourgeoisie, and her exacerbated sense of responsibility seem to have crystallized around this death. Had Zaza not died it is possible to imagine that Simone de Beauvoir would not have carried with her, after her adolescent liberation, such strong feelings of revolt. Nor would she perhaps have felt so deeply the need to bear witness, through literature, to her own life and that of her generation. Zaza's death was the social evil that no triumph could erase. The evil had to be accounted for, responsibility attributed, and the guilty indicted.

The four quotations from "Anne," the fourth of the five *récits* in "La Primauté du spirituel," are inferior in quality to similar passages in the *Mémoires d'une jeune fille rangée,* but they are more explicit, particularly the last and longest. Anne is the fictional name for Zaza in "La Primauté du spirituel." The title of this unpublished work is an ironic reminder of Jacques Maritain's *La Primauté du spirituel* (1926), a defense of the idea of a Christian democracy. In Simone de Beauvoir's *récits* the young women, with the exception of Marguerite, the heroine of the last *récit,* succumb mentally or physically to the conflicts and the "bad faith" engendered by their milieu and their desperate, ineffectual attempts to liberate themselves from it. They are particularly susceptible, like the characters in Mary McCarthy's *The Group,* to the frustrations, tensions, and hysteria that emanate from sexual taboos. "In my family we always gave priority to spiritual values," [8] says Marguerite, the sole, lucid survivor. The "priority" of the "spiritual"—the false idols, the "belles images"—leads to despair, sterility and death. Anne is the exemplary victim—Marguerite, who liberates herself from her family, her God, and her lover, is the exemplary heroine. Her victory is less convincing than Anne's defeat.

Anne's death is reported to us by Pascal, the young man whom she loved and who loved her badly, that is, spiritually; by her mother who loved her in the same way, and by her friend Chantal, the teacher-writer of the "group." Chantal stands in the same relation to Anne in "La Primauté du spirituel" as Simone de Beauvoir does to Zaza in the last pages of the *Mémoires d'une jeune fille rangée*. In both cases what is most important is the effect of the friend's death on the survivor. There is, however, an important difference. In "La Primauté du spirituel" Anne's death is not preceded by the intense love and friendship that exists between Simone de Beauvoir and Zaza in the memoirs.

The three shorter quotations contain three different reactions to Anne's death. The first, Pascal's, and the third, Anne's mother's, are obvious evasions. The second, Chantal's response, suggests a courageous lucidity.

Pascal's reactions are not surprising. He is a pious, pretentious young man, dangerously sentimental, who has, in fact, little inclination either for the kisses of Anne alive or for the sight of Anne dead. Whatever happens to Pascal he transforms into a tale of spiritual enrichment. He profits from all encounters, including the encounter with his fiancée's death. There is a bitter contrast between Pascal's concern with his inner life, Madame Vignon's faith in God's glory, and the reality of the dead girl: "sallow and skeletal." For Pascal and for Madame Vignon death is immediately assimilated into a pre-existing mythology. It is a surprise—unexpected, and troubling—but it is not a serious emotional or metaphysical challenge. Nothing can break through their "bad faith."

Chantal, on the contrary, is aware of the way in which Pascal and Madame Vignon have killed Anne by loving her badly and have used Anne's death for their own self-aggrandizement and justification. She appears to make a supreme effort to see death for what it is: a destructive enemy that came and always comes too soon. In reaction to the false image of Anne perpetuated by Pascal and Madame Vignon, Chantal, in the fourth quotation, proposes to revive, in a book, Anne "as she really was, a being of flesh and fervor." And yet, as Chantal develops in her mind the kind of book she will write, lucidity begins to fade, and in its place appears, as earlier and more blatantly with Pascal and Madame Vignon, a blindness to anything that is exterior to Chantal's personal needs and fears, her egocentric inner life. From the moment Chantal thinks "she had a mission to fulfill in behalf of the pathetic young girl," her anguish in the face of death and Anne's pitiful defeat cease to be essential. They are replaced or quickly transformed into the themes of literary vocation and moral responsibility. Anne no longer occupies the center of the stage. Chantal is now director, actor, spectator; she feeds on Anne's tragic death. The "mission to be fulfilled"—and the vocabulary tells us that Chantal, like Pascal and Madame Vignon, is under the evil spell of the priority of the spiritual—is not a mission to Anne but to herself. At last Chantal has a past, "something that belonged only to her and that others could envy," "a beautiful and tragic story," "her secret," "this magnificent burden." She can become not only a writer, but a mysterious and seductive woman as well. There is something monstrous in her final "I shall never forget you"; it is as if she were thanking her pot of gold.

Chantal practices a double evasion because she can use Anne's death to her own advantage in more than one way. She can move from this death to words and literature; she can at the same time appropriate, for her inner life, the resonances and ramifications of Anne's death.

The account of Zaza's death is significantly different in the

Mémoires d'une jeune fille rangée. The death is reported and recorded, a fortunate aesthetic choice which reflects an awareness of the past failure in presenting this scene. In the first paragraph the moments follow each other with a simple and inevitable precision. Zaza's pathetic lucidity "and knew then that she was going to die" conveys something of what dying is perhaps all about.

In the second paragraph the same uncluttered simplicity is maintained. As in "Anne" the contrast between the description of the dead girl and her father's words (in "Anne" they were spoken by the mother) kill God more surely than the best-wrought intellectual argument. The end of the concluding paragraph presents a serious and crucial problem. The ambiguous medical diagnosis and the narrator's recurrent dream, seemingly unrelated, do indeed represent a question and an answer. The nature of Zaza's malady is incidental. What matters is that she died and that her friend survived. The guilt dream is fairly common among chief mourners, and Simone de Beauvoir clearly feels guilty. Feelings of guilt lead to feelings of responsibility, and responsibility often leads to action. Responsibility and action tend to be, in the world of Simone de Beauvoir, evasions in the guise of solutions.

With the last sentence of the passage quoted pompous rhetoric and obvious prevarication return. The need to generalize on the basis of "and seeming to gaze reproachfully at me" destroys the impact of the specific event. "I had paid for my own freedom with her death" is, as with Chantal, a means of using Zaza's death so as to give the narrator an importance, a prestige she would otherwise not have known. Zaza's death is replaced by the narrator's freedom. In all fairness it must be noted that these are the last words of the *Mémoires d'une jeune fille rangée* and that it is only proper that the narrator herself should be the subject of these words. But their effect is to obliterate Zaza's death in particular and death in general. Because of this death the narrator is free. Because of this death the narrator writes. Zaza, too, finally is immolated so that her loving friend may prosper. The horror of death is replaced by a moral debt which in itself is a *raison d'être*. To write in order to redeem Zaza means that Zaza is not dead. Zaza lives.

But Anne-Zaza is dead. So are Louise's baby, Uncle Maurice, Uncle Gaston, and both grandfathers. Others do die. In these early encounters with death, Simone de Beauvoir seems to have fortified herself against the horror. When a particular person dies, death can be condoned. It can be used to condemn society, to verify nature's laws, to strengthen a love relationship, to inspire the writer and make her more interesting. When she herself is concerned, as with the old jacket or the death of God, the anguish is unalleviated. Only Simone de Beauvoir really dies.

CHAPTER VI

Death and the Occupation

In Vienna, under the amused glances of the passers-by, the Jews were cleaning the pavements with acids that ate into their fingers. We weren't going to get ourselves killed for that; nor to stop, almost every night in Prague, the muffled shots of the suicides; nor to prevent the fires that would soon be lit in the Polish villages. While we were busied in stating reasons why we did not wish to die, did we bother about discovering why we were still alive?

The Blood of Others [1]

We did not dare to kill, we did not want to die, and those gray-green vermin devour our living bodies. Women and newborn children die in the ditches; on the soil that is already no longer ours, a huge steel net has fallen, caging Frenchmen by the million. Because of me. "Each of us is responsible for everything." One night, under the piano, he had dug his nails into the carpet, and that bitter thing had been in his throat; but he was only a child, he had wept and gone to sleep.

Ibid. [2]

The woman was standing motionless in the middle of the square. The bus moved off heavily.

"Ruth! Ruth!" She stretched out her hands and started to run after the bus. She was wearing sandals with high, worn heels and she ran in clumsy jerks. A policeman followed her with great masculine strides, in no apparent hurry. She shouted: "Ruth!"

once more, a strident, despairing cry. Then she stopped at the corner of the street and put her head in her hands. The little square was quite quiet, and she was there, in the middle of a blue Sunday, her head in her hands, and her heart breaking. The policeman put his hand on her shoulder.

"Oh, why? Why?" thought Hélène with despair. She was weeping but she remained motionless like the others and she was watching. She was there and her presence made no difference. She crossed the square. "As if I did not exist. And yet I exist. I exist in my locked room, I exist in space. I do not matter. Is it my fault?" In front of the Pantheon, some German soldiers were getting out of a touring car; they looked somewhat tired, they did not resemble those spirited victors who shouted "Heil!" on the roads. "I was watching the march of History! It was my personal history. All that is happening to me."

Ibid.[3]

"I'm no longer afraid." She felt light and fully herself as on the finest evenings of her childhood, when she rested in the arms of a paternal God. To be dead; one is never dead. There is no one left to be dead. I am alive. I shall always be alive. She felt her life beat in her breast and that moment was eternal.

Ibid.[4]

We could throw ourselves against the Duke's army, burn our houses and all die together.

Les Bouches inutiles [5]

A freely chosen death is not an evil. But these women and old men whom you are going to throw into the ravine have no choice. You are cheating them of their death as well as their life. We shall not do that. Tonight, united in a single purpose, may a free people face its destiny.

Ibid.[6]

"Our torturers gave us very bad habits," wrote Gracchus Babeuf regretfully. Under the Nazi oppression, faced with the traitors who were their accomplices, we too developed in our hearts venomous feelings we had never known before. . . .

Since June 1940 we have learned anger and hate. We longed for the humiliation and the death of our enemies. And today, each time that a court condemns a war criminal, an informer, a collaborationist, we feel responsible for the verdict. . . . We congratulated ourselves when Mussolini died, when the assassins of Kharkov were hanged, when Darnand wept: in this way we participated in their condemnation. Their crimes touched us deeply; our values, our reasons for living are reinforced by their punishment.

"Oeil pour oeil," in *L'Existentialisme
et la sagesse des nations* [7]

A soldier who kills in combat is not detestable because he is obeying orders and because there is reciprocity in the situation that exists between him and his adversary; neither death, nor suffering, nor captivity are in themselves scandalous. Scandal erupts only at the moment when a man treats his fellowmen like objects, when he denies them—through tortures, humiliation, slavery, assassination—their right to exist as men.

Ibid.[8]

We were frustrated by Hitler's death; we had hoped that he would remain alive and aware of his fall, that he would "understand." The ideal vengeance is the one that Louis XI wrought on La Balue, or Judex on the evil banker whom he imprisoned for life in a cell. In these cases a human consciousness is present and prisoner of the situation imposed on it; it is fixed in despair, although there is always the possibility of evasion into madness.

Ibid.[9]

And in his box, alone, cut off from everyone, there was a man who had been elevated by circumstances to his greatest height. He was placed face to face with his death and therefore with his entire life which he was obliged to assume in the face of death. Whatever his life had been, whatever the reasons for his death, his dignified behavior in this extreme situation demanded our respect at a time when we would have most liked to despise him. We desired the death of the editor of *Je suis partout*, not the death of this man so eager to die well.

Ibid.[10]

Tonight's a holiday, the first Christmas of peace, the last Christmas at Buchenwald, the last Christmas on earth, the first

Christmas Diego hasn't lived through. We were dancing, we were kissing each other around the tree sparkling with promises, and there were many, oh, so many, who weren't there. No one had heard their last words; they were buried nowhere, swallowed up in emptiness. Two days after the liberation, Geneviève had placed her hand on a coffin. Was it the right one? Jacques' body had never been found; a friend claimed he had buried his notebooks under a tree. What notebooks? Which tree? Sonia had asked for a sweater and silk stockings and then she never again asked for anything. Where were Rachel's bones and the lovely Rosa's? In the arms that had so often clasped Rosa's soft body, Lambert was now holding Nadine, and Nadine was laughing the way she used to laugh when Diego held her in his arms. I looked down the row of Christmas trees reflected in the large mirrors and I thought, "There are the candles and the holly and the mistletoe they'll never see. Everything that's been given me, I stole from them." They were killed. Which one first? He or his father? Death didn't enter into his plans. Did he know he was going to die? Did he rebel at the end or was he resigned to it? How will I ever know? And now that he's dead, what difference does it make? . . . The dead are dead; for them there are no more problems. But after this night of festivity, we, the living, will awaken again. And then how shall we live?

The Mandarins [11]

I was shattered, both by Lise's grief and on my own account. There had been plenty of other deaths to sicken me, but this one touched me intimately. Bourla had been a close neighbor of mine, and I had taken him to my heart: besides, he was only nineteen. Sartre did his best to convince me that in a sense *every* life is complete at its end, and that death at nineteen is fundamentally no more absurd than death at eighty; but I did not believe him. . . . there was no grave, no body, not even so much as a bone. It was as though nothing had happened, absolutely nothing. . . . This nothingness terrified me. . . . He had not gone to his death willingly; it had come to him without his consent. Had he stood for an instant and seen his end, looked death in the face? And who had been the first to go, he or his father? If he was conscious, I felt certain he must have cried *No!*, aloud or in his heart, a last frantic, terrible spasm that was all for nothing—and remained thus, rooted in eternity. He had cried *No!*, and then there had been—nothing. I found the very thought unbearable; but I had to bear it. . . . For a few months I had felt myself reviving, with a new lease on life hung dazzlingly before me. But now Bourla was gone. Never before had I been brought up against the ghastly uncertainty of our mortal state in so irrefutable a way. . . . Because of his death and all it signified, my moments of agony and despair reached an intensity I had never known, which could only be described as hellish. But no sooner had I shaken off this mood than I was caught up by glorious visions of the future and by all the diverse elements that went into the fabric of my daily happiness.

The Prime of Life [12]

And as a matter of fact, if it is true that men seek in the future a guarantee of their success, a negation of their failures, it is true that they also feel the need of denying the indefinite flight of time and of holding their present between their hands. Existence must be asserted in the present if one does not want all life to be defined as an escape toward nothingness. That is the reason societies institute festivals whose role is to stop the movement of transcendence, to set up the end as an end. The hours following the liberation of Paris, for example, were an immense collective festival exalting the happy and absolute end of that particular history which was precisely the occupation of Paris. . . . One of art's roles is to fix this passionate assertion of existence in a more durable way: the festival is at the origin of the theater, music, the dance, and poetry. In telling a story, in depicting it, one makes it exist in its particularity with its beginning and its end, its glory or its shame; and this is the way it actually must be lived. In the festival, in art, men express their need to feel that they exist absolutely. They must really fulfill this wish. What stops them is that as soon as they give the word "end" its double meaning of goal and fulfillment they clearly perceive this ambiguity of their condition, which is the most fundamental of all: that every living movement is a sliding toward death. But if they are willing to look it in the face they also discover that every movement toward death is life. In the past people cried out, "The king is dead, long live the king"; thus the present must die so that it may live; existence must not deny this death which it carries in its heart but will this death; it must assert itself as an absolute in its very finiteness; man fulfills himself within the transitory or not at all. He must regard his undertakings as finite and will them absolutely.

The Ethics of Ambiguity [13]

Approximately forty million inhabitants of our planet were killed or died—on the battlefields, in the air, on the sea, in concentration and prison camps, in villages and cities—during the years of the Second World War. Of these forty million or so, some six hundred and eighteen thousand were French. The French dead were mainly victims of the German occupation: deported Jews, political prisoners, members of the Resistance. The fighting war for France, with the exception of the Second Armored Division under General Jacques Philippe Leclerc and the group under General Marie-Pierre Koenig, was tragically and mercifully short.

Whatever the circumstances of a human death, the outcome is the same. The attitudes towards death, however, among the living and the dying, change considerably under certain circumstances. During a war it is easier to give a meaning to death; it is easier to speak convincingly of solidarity and fraternity; it is possible to give death a moral dimension and, even for atheists, a transcendent value.

War, although it dramatically increases the number of the dead and the possibility of dying, masks the reality of death. It makes evasion acceptable, inevitable. Specifically, war obliges even the most solitary individual to move out from the universe of refined individualism into some contact, some participation with a collectivity. Participation always diminishes anguish and in time of war the "horror of death" frequently gives way to the more tolerable "chance of death." [14] There are always fewer suicides during a war. The tortured intellectual is more at home with death in a period of catastrophic national or international crisis than in the calmer, lonelier, periods of relative peace. This was eminently true of Sartre and Simone de Beauvoir during the

Algerian War and the baffling events of May 1968. It is difficult to fight against the human condition; the revolt tends to become abstract. It is easier and exhilarating to fight against an imposed situation. For Sartre, the vital experience was the months spent in a prisoner-of-war camp in Germany. Even before his imprisonment he drew conclusions from his experience as a soldier that were immediately accepted, intellectually at least, by Simone de Beauvoir:

> Sartre was thinking a good deal about the postwar period; he had firmly made up his mind to hold aloof from politics no longer. His new morality was based on the notion of "genuineness," and he was determined to make a practical application of it to himself. It required every man to shoulder the responsibility of his situation in life; and the only way in which he could do so was to transcend that situation by engaging upon some course of action. Any other attitude was mere escapist pretense, a masquerade based upon insincerity. It will be clear that a radical change had taken place in him—and in me too, since I rallied to his point of view immediately; for not so long ago our first concern had been to keep our situation in life at arm's length by means of fantasy, deception, and plain lies.[15]

What is essentially involved here is the crucial drama of Sartre's intellectual life: the awareness of conditioning and the dogged attempt to maintain, in the face of this awesome conditioning, a measure of freedom by making the state of war, that is, action, a perpetual state.

The works conceived and in great part written by Simone de Beauvoir during the war years, *Pyrrhus et Cinéas, Le Sang des autres, Les Bouches inutiles, Tous les Hommes sont mortels* and her "Journal de Guerre," all reveal the moral, didactic bias, the terrible seriousness, explicit in Sartre's new attitude. In the essay as well as the works of fiction, nihilism and solitude are unconvincingly vanquished by some form of collective action. The dread of death succumbs to the power of the cause—socialism, the Resistance—and to the effective dialectic between guilt and responsibility.

The decision to act remains a theoretical decision. Simone de Beauvoir arranges and observes the consequences of action in the behavior of her characters. She lived through the years of the Occupation in a very different style from that of her heroes and heroines; different also from that of an active minority of her countrymen and women. Her "Journal de guerre" shows her doing the same things she had always done: reading, writing, listening to music, talking to Sartre, going on walking trips and bicycle trips, teaching, skiing, becoming famous (at least after the publication of *L'Invitée* in 1943) and enthusiastically making new and famous acquaintances with whom she and Sartre celebrate the "festas" of 1944. Death is all around her, rarely near by. Something is always happening to someone else: to foreigners, to Jews, to Communists, to active Resistance fighters. Except for the separation from Sartre at the beginning of the war, Simone de Beauvoir remains outside the serious, immediate sufferings and catastrophes. She chooses her participation; it is minimal. She is anti-Nazi, anti-Vichy, pro-Resistance. These attitudes do not involve any direct action on her part. What is still more important is that in this whirl of deliberate *divertissement*, she is rarely alone. The "we" that refers to Simone de Beauvoir and Sartre is a constant pronoun during these years.

If no document existed concerning the Occupation of France other than Simone de Beauvoir's "Journal de guerre" and the second volume of her memoirs, *La Force de l'âge*, written fifteen years after the war and in which the "Journal de guerre" is inserted, the image we would have of these years would correspond quite faithfully, in its general lines, to the reality lived through by most adult Parisians. These Parisians, like Simone de Beauvoir, saw certain of their neighbors disappear, heard about the camps without ever really knowing what was going on in them, knew of men and women who had been killed by the Gestapo, knew a few Jews, saw the Nazi flags flying and the German soldiers strutting. More intimately they knew the food and clothing shortages, the increasingly dowdy living conditions, the occasional pangs of guilt and bouts of fear. Their main efforts were devoted to surviving with their family or close friends, and they did. Their imaginations, like Simone de Beauvoir's, conjure up horrors that relate to themselves and their loved ones; rarely to those who are in fact dying and suffering.

Simone de Beauvoir imagines her own nothingness, Sartre's disappearance, and she suffers keenly. Otherwise her imagination is quite barren:

. . . At the end of June the first rockets fell on London. They dropped at random, without any warning of their arrival; at any moment you could imagine that some dearly loved friend had just been killed. This vague, omnipresent insecurity seemed to me the worst possible sort of ordeal, and I dreaded the thought that I might one day be called upon to face it myself.

But for the present we remained in ignorance of this. We went for walks and had drinks together and discussed things.[16]

There is nothing either to judge or to condemn here. There is no reason not to walk, drink, and talk since the bombs were falling elsewhere. And as Sartre had said to Simone de Beauvoir: "it is possible to live in great tranquility even at a time when your life is hedged about with danger." [17]

As passage after passage relates the suffering of others and the survival techniques of Simone de Beauvoir, the reader begins to feel a certain uneasiness in the excessive preoccupation with what "I" did while it was all going on. Still more irritating is the constant, pathological need to be where the action is and not to miss anything important. At times one wonders if anything important ever happens when Simone de Beauvoir and Sartre are not there to bear witness. She looked forward to the liberation of Paris in the same way a young child waits for Christmas. It was to be for her the ultimate fete and the ultimate evasion: "we had no wish to miss the actual Liberation," [18] she wrote in July of 1944. One has the unpleasant feeling that it is all being done as a recompense to her for having survived.

The most rewarding moments for the reader in the "Journal de guerre" and the *Force de l'âge* are those in which Simone de Beauvoir alternately knows about death and forgets what she knows or that she knows. This capriciousness of the mind, its apparent inability to fix for any length of time its attention on one image or idea—particularly if it is disturbing—the ease with which it can be, indeed asks to be, distracted, is the essential factor in the constant seesaw between awareness and evasion. More than just "bad faith" is involved in this process, which seems to tell us as much about the physiology of the mind as about its conditioned betrayals. But, of course, there is always "bad faith," there is always deliberate bamboozlement, which, with Simone de Beauvoir, often accompanies an ostensibly lucid analysis.

Till war broke out I had followed my own bent, learning about the world and constructing a private pattern of happiness. Morality became identified in my mind with pursuits such as these: it was indeed my Golden Age. . . . But from 1939 onward, everything changed. The world became a place of chaos, and my work of construction stopped altogether. My one recourse was the verbal exorcism implicit in abstract moral judgments: I sought desperately for reasons or formulae that would justify me in enduring the lot now thrust upon me. I found one or two in which I still have faith; I learned about human solidarity, and personal responsibilities, and the fact that it was possible to accept death in order that life might keep a meaning. But these truths I learned, in a way, against my natural inclinations. I used words to talk myself into accepting them. I expounded them to myself, I turned my powers of persuasion inward and gave myself a regular lesson. It was this lesson I now strove to pass on, ignoring the fact that it might not come as freshly to the reader as it had come to me.[19]

Simone de Beauvoir is criticizing the overbearing moralism of her works written during the Occupation. What is the value of this self-criticism? She is trying to tell us why certain of her works were unsuccessful. Her analysis appears valid. The truths that she discovered during the war were contrary to her sensibility; her only means of assimilating these truths was through words. She wrote to convince herself and she failed to convince the reader. What she does in fact tell us is that she never succeeded in convincing herself. The bamboozling words in the paragraph are that she found some in which she still believed and "in order that life might keep a meaning . . . these truths." The "reasons" and "formulae" are transformed into "truths."

Simone de Beauvoir has done exactly the same thing in this paragraph of self-criticism that she did in the works she is criticizing. This discrepancy between words and feelings is the result of a subterfuge. In order to avoid the "chaos" Simone de Beauvoir clings to words. She says: "my work of construction stopped altogether," but words are in themselves constructs. She used "solidarity," "responsibilities," "accept death," "in order that life might keep a meaning" and she fancied that a whole new world of values existed; in fact they were words. The "chaos" alone was real.

The texts that illustrate, in greater detail, death and the Occupation reveal a similar tension between awareness and evasion.

The first, from *Le Sang des autres*, is part of an interior monologue pursued by the hero, Jean, immediately following the Munich appeasement. The passage contains a real and a false problem. The real problem is how an individual or a collectivity should act when another or others are being inhumanly treated. The problem is complicated by the fact that action here necessarily involves violence, that is to say death. The false problem, and it is the false problem that interests Simone de Beauvoir and her characters, is to discover reasons "why we were still alive." These reasons, as they are invented in the course of the novel and in the other works written during this period, obscure the real problem and constitute a logically constructed subterfuge. There can be no absolute reasons for living or dying, only temporary reasons that emerge from a particular situation.

The second quotation, again a part of the hero's interior monologue, raises the same false problem and proposes the beginning of an answer. The evil is now closer to home. Earlier it was the Jews, the Poles, the Czechs. Now it is the French army that is defeated and France itself invaded. The terrible guilt that Jean feels is the same guilt he knew as a child after the death of Louise's baby. The guilt is double. He feels guilty because the outrageous event takes place—the death of Louise's baby, the invasion of France—and he feels guilty because of his own inaction, because he forgets his initial guilt. This guilt will be assuaged and justified by the notion of responsibility. "Each of us is responsible for everything" is the phrase upon which Jean and his creator will build their *raisons d'être*. An ethics of responsibility is an obvious solution to the anguish of guilt. But as the solution is worked out it becomes more and more an abstract intellectual construct; its bearing on any real situation less and less relevant. That is when *moralisme* and *didactisme* invade Simone de Beauvoir's novels and plays.

The reporter of the third quotation is Hélène, the selfish, spoiled young woman who will find, at the very end of the novel and of her life, a meaning for her life and death in Jean's Resistance group. This scene, which precipitates her conversion to collective action, occurs at the moment when the Germans begin the deportation of French Jews. It is one of the most moving and pathetic scenes in the novel. A mother has been separated from her child. The children are in a slowly moving bus; behind them is the mother with her jerky, useless gestures; behind her is the policeman, sure of himself and of the woman's helplessness. The child's name, Ruth, adds a biblical dimension to the scene. It evokes not only Ruth and Naomi, Ruth and Boaz, but a long history of persecution and tears.

The mother's helplessness and despair are felt by Hélène in

terms of guilt and responsibility. Curiously but not surprisingly, Hélène is more upset by the feelings that have been aroused in her and by the problem they pose than by the absolute misery of the woman. Hélène will join the Resistance in order to resolve her own problem: "Why?" "Is it my fault?" "All that is happening to me." She will act in order to feel that she exists. The insistence on the tired-looking German soldier suggests the evolution of a situation; reality is constantly changing. Hélène's imminent participation, we are encouraged to believe, will hasten the change.

The fourth quotation from *Le Sang des autres* presents the optimum solution to the false problem. Hélène, before leaving on the mission, during which she will be mortally wounded, finds the same peace and security, the same absence of fear she knew as a child. The "fatherly God" of the Christians has been replaced by a belief in action, in participation which confers eternity on the moment. Death is unconvincingly dismissed. There is something ludicrously infantile in the insistence on the obvious: "one is never dead." It hardly seems worthwhile to have gone through so much to come out with so little. What troubles the reader is that the ecstatic moment refers to childhood and Christianity. The false problem has received a false solution. The evasion is perfect.

The two short quotations from Simone de Beauvoir's only play, *Les Bouches inutiles*, proposes a similar solution to a similar problem. The city of Vaucelles in Flanders, during the fourteenth century, is besieged by the Burgundians and incapable of withstanding the siege. The final exemplary decision involves the entire community in an act of solidarity which will confer a meaning on the life and the death of the inhabitants of Vaucelles. They will, all together, participate in a collective effort which is almost certain to lead to collective death. Dying together, like dying for one's country, makes death more acceptable. It is an answer to the fear of death and, in the context of this play, to the awesome options of life. Another false resolution and facile evasion.

The extracts from the essay "Oeil pour oeil" must be read in the light of the frenzy of righteous vengeance and violence that seized many Frenchmen in the months following the liberation of France. The death of the enemy—the Fascists of all countries but particularly the collaborators—was longed for. It is not difficult to understand these passionate reactions. What is disconcerting is their verbal justification and the leap from feeling to rationalization and ideology. Any form of racism, any desire to kill would, in like manner, be made to seem proper.

Simone de Beauvoir's intransigence and her apology for violence in "Oeil pour oeil" are possible precisely because the reality of death is so consistently evaded. Death is envisaged as a means of humiliation, retribution, vengeance, poetic justice. Only in the last extract when she speaks of Robert Brasillach, whom she saw in person when she attended his trial, does she come close to a sense of human reality. And, at the same time, she exposes the major weakness in her blood-thirsty argument. "We desired the death of the editor of *Je suis partout*, not the death of this man so eager to die well." But the editor-in-chief of *Je suis partout* was and could only be a man, as Mussolini, Darnand, Hitler, Balue, and the assassins of Kharkov were men. The sense of a common humanity only seldom touches Simone de Beauvoir; when it does she writhes in anguish. Her inability to relate to people with whom she is not intimate prevents her from feeling for them. She is protected from exposure to reality by the words she has previously chosen to describe that reality.

The death during the Occupation that had the greatest effect on Simone de Beauvoir was that of Bourla, a young Spanish Jewish poet, and a member of the "family." Bourla was the lover of Lise, an ex-student and a close friend of Simone de Beauvoir's. He was nineteen when he was arrested, imprisoned, and shot. The incident is recounted in the *Force de l'âge* and in *Les Mandarins*. In *Les Mandarins* the death of Bourla-Diego is felt more strongly than any other by Anne, one of the two major protagonists in the novel.

Why does Diego's death occupy this privileged position? Because Anne knew him well. He was her daughter's lover and at
night she would tuck them into bed and kiss them. Because he
was a poet, and very young and full of life. Because the facts
surrounding his death were not known; because there was no
body—only emptiness and absence. The manner of Bourla-Diego's
death corresponds to Simon de Beauvoir's personal horror of
nothingness; total disappearance as if the living person had never
been. "Nothing will have taken place." And, finally, because it is
possible to feel guilt. "Everything that's been given me, I stole
from them" is echoed in Simone de Beauvoir's sense of guilt when
Zaza dies. Guilt turns the human being in on himself and away
from death; guilt facilitates evasion. Nevertheless the question
Anne asks at the end of this passage, "how shall we live?"—the
subject of *Les Mandarins*—is really the question of how to live
with death, with those who are already dead and those who have
yet to die; how to live with the fact and the awareness of death.
Diego's death is one of the events that Anne's intellectual structures cannot easily absorb. It operates as a catalyst, in the course
of the novel, for her circuitous meditation on death.

The passage in *La Force de l'âge* ends on a characteristic note:
"But no sooner had I shaken off this mood." Despair, death, the
very elements that compose our human condition are regarded
as unpleasant, always unforeseen, intruders. Again no attempt is
made to explore death or to consider seriously Sartre's remark:
"death at nineteen is fundamentally no more absurd than death
at eighty." The anguish is so intense that the mind rushes off on
the first possible side road.

The ultimate escape from death and the Occupation is the lyrical apotheosis of the fete, and the Liberation of Paris is the fete
of fetes. "Nocturnal fetes in honor of young love, gigantic fetes
. . . : beneath the lively wine-flown raptures [*ivresses vivantes*]
there is always a faint taste of death, but for one resplendent

moment death is reduced to nothingness." [20] In the context of the
first two volumes of the memoirs, the fete establishes a link between Simone de Beauvoir's religious ecstasies as a child, her joy-
ous reunion with Zaza, as a young woman her initial enchantment
with bars and alcohol, her supreme pleasure in the "festas"
held during the last year of the Occupation, the sensual fetes of
love and the essence of her literary vocation. In each case what
is fundamental is the ecstatic instant which destroys time—the
past and the future—and therefore, ultimately death. The timeless
ecstatic instant contains the possibility of communion with the
universe, with others, with the self.

In *Tous les Hommes sont mortels* the key word of the novel
is fete. Mortal men, as opposed to the immortal Fosca, are always
celebrating their ephemeral victories with fetes. When Simone de
Beauvoir, in *La Force des choses*, attacks the new novelists, it is
precisely because, in their universe, there can be no fete. "But on
the whole, one of the constant factors of this whole school of
writing is boredom; it takes all the savour, all the fire out of life,
its impulse towards the future. Sartre defined literature as a celebration [*fête*]: joyful or tragic, but a celebration [*fête*]; we're a
far cry from that! It is a dead world they are building, these
disciples of the new school." [21] This criticism is specious. The
opposition between fete and "dead world" is postulated in the
same way as the good-evil dichotomy. The new novelists are condemned for epistemological reasons which are never analyzed but
are stated in emotional terms.

In the world of Simone de Beauvoir the Liberation of Paris on
the twenty-fifth of August 1944 occupies a special place. "Seldom
indeed does one achieve a long-awaited pleasure and find it all
one could have hoped for; but such was my good fortune on this
occasion." [22] The Liberation was *the* fete, an individual and collective celebration, the culmination of ardent yearning and desperate hope; the magic moment that vindicated suffering and
death. There can be no question that the twenty-fifth of August
1944 was a day of delirious joy. It was a historic moment. But

Simone de Beauvoir has made of it a sacred moment, the zenith of solidarity and fraternity to which she returns constantly for metaphysical, psychological, and political reassurance. Because there was the Liberation, the Occupation is redeemed and a new world is possible; because there was a fete, "death for one resplendent moment is reduced to nothingness." A real event, a unique event, becomes the unstable foundation of a dangerous myth from which death is categorically excluded. Simone de Beauvoir's fete, like the Christian paradise, is based on the self-defeating principle of exclusion. If the fete implied an acceptance of the fact of death there would not be the sudden sense of failure and emptiness that periodically and increasingly seizes Simone de Beauvoir and most of her characters. Nor would there be the terrible sense of guilt.

The first part of an earlier passage on the fete from *Pour une morale de l'ambiguité* describes the fete as an answer to "the need of denying the indefinite flight of time." As an affirmation of the present the fete, whether it be the liberation of Paris or a form of art, is a revolt against death. Death and time are synonymous. But in the second and final part of the passage the argument changes; it becomes more complex. "Existence must not deny this death which it carries in its heart, but will this death." Death is recognized and immediately transformed from an evil to a good. This sudden and unexpected conversion of values is as excessive and dangerous as the earlier evasions. In a serious attempt to describe the human condition, the injunction to will death is an empty moral imperative; so is "He must regard his undertakings as finite and will them absolutely." A need for verbal and metaphysical order has taken precedence over any real attempt to "look it (death) in the face."

"Death stalked among us daily, and it was impossible to think of anything else," [23] wrote Simone de Beauvoir in *La Force de l'âge*, referring to the period at the end of May 1940. And towards the end of the same volume, in her résumé of the importance of the years 1939–1944 she writes: "Never did my own death and the death of others obsess me so violently as during those years." [24] Simone de Beauvoir's attitude toward death does not undergo any significant change during the Occupation. Those of her friends and acquaintances who were killed, with the exception of Bourla and perhaps the Communist and writer Paul Nizan, were considered in a political-historical perspective, not as dead men. Indeed, until the very last pages of *La Force de l'âge*, death, during the Occupation, seems infinitely less frightful than the confrontation with the old jacket, with the death of God, with the death of Zaza. The reasons for this are understandable. Essentially death in war is fortuitous. It does not have the implacable tragic nature of inevitability. Since it is an accident there are explanations and justifications.

There is a change, however, during this period in Simone de Beauvoir's attitude towards her own death. The anguish, when it comes, is increasingly intense. The moments of crisis resemble severe pathological states, or mystical trances. These moments tend to be precipitated by solitude, by too much alcohol, and by any unusually difficult situation. All of Simone de Beauvoir's emotional energy is directed towards the dread of her own death. It is not therefore surprising that during the Occupation this anguish should have increased. An important factor is her age and her consciousness of her age. Simone de Beauvoir suffers from an excoriating sense of the years that have been lived, that are left to live; what one does and does not do at a certain age. At thirty Simone de Beauvoir felt that she was old. This insistence on her lost youth and approaching age is a central preoccupation in her works that come after the war.

". . . Despite all the deaths that lay behind me, despite all my anger and rebelliousness, I had re-established myself in the condition of happiness. Of all the blows I had endured, none had broken me. I had survived; indeed I was unscathed." [25] In spite of the violence of the crises that occasionally overwhelmed Simone de Beauvoir she survived the occupation years buoyantly. The reason is in part physiological. Simone de Beauvoir was a young and middle-aged woman of tremendous vitality and endurance. Her walking and bicycle trips attest to an unusual stamina. If she was more resilient than most people it may quite simply be because her health was exceptionally good. Another reason may perhaps be linked to the fact that Simone de Beauvoir, in spite of her professed atheism, tends to be a believer. In a period of catastrophe belief in the future is essential to survival. During the Occupation she believed in Sartre, in the future, in history. As long as Sartre was alive the future was open and history was inevitable.

Simone de Beauvoir survived more successfully during the war than in the years that followed. Death under the Occupation was easy to rationalize, and therefore to evade. After 1944 death was no longer all around her, it was increasingly inside. Ostensibly history and commitment, commitment to violence, had replaced anguish in the formulation of problems. In fact the anguish of the fear of death had gone underground only to emerge more virulent than ever.

CHAPTER VII

The Death of Others:
Deaths in Fiction

Behind Xavière's maniacal pleasure, behind her hatred and jealousy, the abomination loomed, as monstrous and definitive as death. Before Françoise's very eyes, yet apart from her, existed something like a condemnation with no appeal: detached, absolute, unalterable, an alien conscience was rising. . . . Pictures kept flashing through Françoise's mind—an old jacket, a deserted glade, a corner of the Pôle Nord where Pierre and Xavière were carrying on a mysterious tête-à-tête far removed from her. She had felt before, as she did this night, her own being dissolving itself in favor of other inaccessible beings; but never had she realized with such perfect lucidity her own annihilation.

She Came to Stay [1]

From Vassieux to Hiroshima—they had gone a long way in a single year. The next war would really be something! And the next postwar period, that would be even neater than this one! That is, if there is a next postwar period—if the defeated don't take it into their heads to blow up the world. And it could very well happen. Granted, it wouldn't break into pieces; it would just continue turning on its axis, frozen, barren. But that picture was hardly more cheering. The thought of death had never bothered Henri, but suddenly that lunar silence terrified him. Mankind would be no more! In face of that deaf-and-dumb eternity, what earthly sense was there in setting words on paper, holding meetings? You had only to sit back and silently await the universal

cataclysm, or your own insignificant death. Nothing meant anything.

The Mandarins [2]

"Mama, why do people live?" . . . Such anxiety in the eyes of
this little girl I still treat as though she were a baby. Why does
she ask herself this question? So that is what is making her cry,
then? . . . "But what about the people who aren't happy: why
are they alive?"

"You've seen unhappy people? Where, darling? . . . You can
treat sick people, give poor ones money—there are masses of
things you can do."

"Are there really? For everybody?"

"Dear me, I should cry all day long if there were people whose
unhappiness couldn't be cured at all. Tell me all about it tomorrow. And I promise you we'll find something to be done. I
promise," she repeated, stroking Catherine's hair. "Go to sleep
now, darling."

Les Belles Images [3]

How I cried at my first encounter with death. Then I cried
less and less: my parents, my brother-in-law, my father-in-law,
friends. That, too, is part of getting old. So many dead people
behind you, mourned, forgotten.

"L'Age de discrétion," in *La Femme rompue* [4]

She [her daughter] is dead and so what? The dead aren't saints.
. . . The terrible memory the blue sky all those flowers Albert
in tears in front of people one behaves oneself for heaven's sake.
I behaved myself and yet I knew that this was the last blow. It
was me they buried. I am buried.

"Monologue," in *La Femme rompue* [5]

(Perhaps my father's death is not unrelated to this *laissez-aller*.
Something snapped. I stopped time from that moment on.)

"La Femme rompue," in *La Femme rompue* [6]

An adult does not react to death in the same way as a child,
although the reaction to initial encounters with death may well
establish a pattern of behavior that is repeated when another death

occurs. The essential difference in Simone de Beauvoir's reaction to her encounters with death is that she herself ages and that as she ages she draws closer to her own death. The death of middle-aged contemporaries quite naturally involves an element of identification which is not present to the same degree when older relatives or very young children die.

The adult is perhaps less preoccupied with death than with the particular circumstances that surround the death: who died and how. Dying assumes greater importance. In the category of deaths in fiction and deaths in autobiography are all the deaths that follow Zaza's in Simone de Beauvoir's fictional and autobiographical writings, including those of intimate friends who die during the war and the Occupation of France. The list is moderate in the novels and *récits*, short, as one would expect, in the essays, and long in the memoirs.

In the novels and *récits* the deaths are varied in form and content. There is less reworking of the same incidents—the death of Louise's baby, the death of Zaza—than in the early deaths. The death of Xavière in *L'Invitée* is an abstract death whose function is to illustrate the novel's epigraph, which is taken from Hegel: "Each conscience seeks the death of the other." When, at the end of the book, Françoise kills Xavière by turning on the gas in the sleeping girl's room, we are conscious neither of a real murder nor of a real death. Françoise has annihilated a consciousness. But, despite the deliberately calculated aspect of the death, it contains, symbolically, an important element. When Françoise kills Xavière, what she is really attempting to kill is the intimation of her own nothingness which Xavière's presence reveals. The death of "the other" takes on a very particular meaning. "The other" must be completely destroyed so that Françoise may live.

Françoise kills in order not to be killed, in order not to die. "The other" in the context of *L'Invitée* is death. This definition of "the other" is also a form of evasion. Nothingness and death are replaced by an adversary against whom there is the possibility of combat and of victory. Olga in the second volume of the memoirs and Xavière in *L'Invitée* are projections of Simone de Beauvoir's anguish. But the fundamental anguish is stronger than the substitutes invented to allay it.

The Occupation of France puts death and "the other" in an apparently different perspective. Death by accident becomes a daily occurrence and "the other" becomes a source of guilt and responsibility. In *Le Sang des autres* the death of Hélène, preceded by the death of Louise's baby and the death of Jacques, is a redemptive death. Because Hélène knows why she is dying, her death as a member of Jean's Resistance group has a meaning. For Jean, who reviews his life as he watches her die, Hélène's death provides the courage to continue, to accept guilt and responsibility as the price that must be paid in the fight for freedom. Strangely enough, here too, as in *L'Invitée*, the death of "the other" frees the protagonist. Jean's last words, although different from Françoise's, carry almost the same moral message:

Françoise: It was her own will which was being fulfilled, now nothing separated her from herself. She had chosen at last. She had chosen herself.[7]

Jean: You have given me the courage to accept forever the risk and the anguish, to bear my crimes and my guilt [*remords*], which will rend me eternally. There is no other way.[8]

Both protagonists choose themselves, accept themselves. The death of "the other" is a confrontation with the self which ends in triumph. The dread of death is obliterated. Fundamentally, then, despite the totally different circumstances, there is little change between the death of Xavière and the death of Hélène from the point of view of its effect on the protagonist.

In *Tous les Hommes sont mortels* there are innumerable deaths. Fosca, the hero, born in 1279, is still alive in the twentieth century. For Fosca, the deaths of all those whom he loved and knew, particularly his wives Béatrice and Marianne and his son Antoine, are the events through which he understands the double tragedy of mortality and immortality. Mortals, like Régine, the twentieth-century actress to whom Fosca tells his incredible tale, are haunted by their morality, by the desire to destroy "the other," to "leave a mark," and by the knowledge that they are doomed to nothingness. "I don't want to be a blade of grass" [9] is Régine's reiterated cry. Human beings in *Tous les Hommes sont mortels* are defined by their mortality; it is what gives meaning to their lives. Immortality, at least in the world of mortals, is not the answer to human anguish. Fosca's solitude and his inability to participate in limited human enterprises make of his eternal life an endless boredom. Fosca's ennui is constantly juxtaposed to the successive passions and fetes of mortals. His suffering, his death in life, is made to appear much more intense than that of the mortals whom he encounters, with the exception of Régine.

Tous les Hommes sont mortels tries to tell us that, even if there were no death, the human condition would be intolerable. Death is only one of our limitations and not the most serious: "I shall never be anyone else," [10] laments Fosca. The inability to get out of one's self, which condemns to endless repetition, is the price of immortality. What death gives by contrast is precious: the sense of a unique life; the sense of risk and danger; the desire to live and to act.

There is a partial evasion in the conception of the novel. With the choice of an immortal as hero, the problem of mortality becomes at times as abstract as the murder and death of Xavière in *L'Invitée*. In fact, Régine's anguish is much greater than Fosca's suffering. At the end of the novel and of his story he walks away: "At the moment when the hour began to strike in the belfry she began to shriek." [11] Régine's last cry, the cry of the mortal who does not want to die, is stronger than the weight of the stone Fosca-Sisyphus must eternally push up the hill. For, after all, there are no immortals; all men are mortal. The reader is not convinced by the implicit thesis that death is a blessing. To be convinced would be to adopt the point of view of an immortal man or one who believes in immortality.

Many people die in *Les Mandarins*. The effect of young Diego's death on the protagonist Anne Dubreuil was explored in the preceding chapter. There is, in *Les Mandarins*, another moment when the death of others plays an important role in the development of a character. During a bicycle trip through France, Anne, her husband Robert (the chief mandarin), and Henri, the novel's second protagonist and Anne's alter ego, read about the American atomic bomb attack on Hiroshima. Shortly afterwards they come upon the small town of Vassieux in the Vercors, a center of Resistance activity, which is celebrating its fete in honor of the dead. The dead are the men, women, and children whom the Germans, in acts of reprisal, burned and shot and whom the survivors discuss as they eat and drink with Rabelaisian fervor. Henri's reaction gives a new dimension to the death of others.

Unlike Anne, Henri is not normally preoccupied with death, his own or that of others. What prompts his outburst is the vision of the destruction of humanity, of the entire human species, an idea which the atomic bomb dropped on Hiroshima suddenly makes possible. The empty planet turning in space gives a cosmic and hallucinating dimension to the more usual concern with personal annihilation. Because Henri is less neurotic than Anne and is not obsessed with his own nothingness, his vision is less egotistical, more fraternal. This is one of the rare moments in the writings of Simone de Beauvoir when an obsession with death includes all men and is thus potentially powerful enough to suggest that a radical change in relation to death would result in a radical change in relation to other people. But this understanding of a common mortality is not explicitly developed. The immediate result of Henri's new awareness is that he writes a play based on the fete in honor of the dead at Vassieux. For Henri the moment of truth becomes a moment of inspiration; he is able to write again. In terms of a real encounter with death, the literary act might well be considered an evasion. Henri, like his creator, turns his momentary suffering into a useful activity. He asks "what earthly sense was there in setting words on paper," but the question is never

seriously considered. Henri writes and the vision of "the world
. . . frozen, barren . . . that lunar silence" disappears. Henri's
anguish is cosmic and universal; his play, which the reader never
reads, is apparently social and local.

In *Les Belles Images* Catherine, the protagonist's ten-year-old
daughter, cries at night because she discovers for herself that human beings are both mortal and unhappy. The "belles images,"
the counterfeit money that circulate in this prosperous, sophisti-
cated, middle-class milieu, are designed to hide or to justify any
form of unhappiness. The only real question in the novel is asked
by the child. Her mother's answers are all the more appalling because they are consciously idiotic. Laurence has been conditioned
to such a degree by her family, she is so afraid of relapsing into
her nervous breakdown of five years ago that she, too, plays the
game of masking reality behind a series of silly, fashionable images.
The entire novel is constructed around the notion of evasion, and
the conclusion, for these characters at least, is that no other road
is open to them. Laurence's important discovery: "in spite of all
the disillusionments, the pretty pictures would remain intact" [12]
does not take her any further than itself. She draws no significant
conclusions from it because she is, like Anne in *Les Mandarins*,
too neurotic, too hopelessly entangled in her own private family
life. There are too many secondary preoccupations; central concerns are cast aside. If, as Catherine does, someone in this milieu
persists in raising disturbing questions, they are threatened with
a psychiatrist; that is to say, answers and justification for erratic
behavior. Simone de Beauvoir is not merely criticizing the bourgeoisie she despises. Consciously or unconsciously she is also
criticizing some of her own evasions. Catherine's questions and
her family's method of coping with them are a synthesized mirror
image of the dialectic that takes place within Simone de Beauvoir.
Like Catherine she asks the fundamental questions; like Laurence
she runs away.

This pathological egotism is accentuated in the three *récits* that
form *La Femme rompue*. In these stories of impending old age

and of failure, the protagonists, all aging women, married and mothers, are much too concerned with their own survival amid the ruins to consider the death of others.

There are significant differences in the attitudes of the three women, differences that mark the milieu, the circumstances and particularly the degree of lucidity of the female voices. The narrator in "L'Age de discrétion" is a wife, a mother, and a writer of the left-wing bourgeoisie, who at the age of sixty has alienated her husband and her son and no longer feels she can write. Her attitude toward death reflects the movement towards indifference that pervades much of what she does. The narrator of the second *récit*, "Monologue," is a woman of forty-three, alone in her apartment on New Year's Eve. She goes over in her troubled mind past events and present feelings. The focal point of the monologue is the suicide of her daughter. The emphasis is on responsibility and vengeance. The dead daughter is a pretext for her mother's hysterical outbursts. In the third *récit*, "La Femme rompue," the narrator Monique discovers that her husband, a successful Parisian doctor, is having a very serious affair with another woman. The discovery destroys her. She suggests that her father's death was responsible for her inability to cope either with her husband or her children.

In the last two cases, the death of the other is used as an excuse for the protagonist's subsequent disintegration. What is important is the effect of the death on the protagonist. Never is the dead or dying person an object of curiosity or concern. These naïvely selfish women manipulate their entourage to the point where manipulation becomes torture. They see themselves as victims; in reality they are killers. Through the composition of the first-person *récit* the author wants the reader to see and feel the "bad faith" of the protagonists. The reader can go one step further from the "bad faith" of the character to the "bad faith" of the author. It is only too easy to condemn these women who tell their story as they choose to tell it. It is more difficult and more pertinent to discover how they have been manipulated by a creator whose own unconscious evasions preclude any real awakening in her characters.

From the death of Xavière in *L'Invitée* to the death of Monique's father in "La Femme rompue," the death of the other in novels and *récits* is presented as an event which divides time into a before and an after. The death always has an enormous impact on the protagonist. It may liberate or enslave, but it never involves an honest encounter, an encounter in which the initial overwhelming anguish is genuinely confronted. The effort is directed towards diminishing the anguish and not towards the exploration of the phenomenon of death.

CHAPTER VIII

The Death of Others: Deaths in Autobiography

People don't speak easily about death in America; you never meet a funeral procession on the street. . . . The pleasant funeral homes situated between a drugstore and a bar give me the shivers; I always expect to see a zombie or a vampire escaping; the reality of death is systematically denied in these places; in the cemeteries you see this reality and that is what gives these gardens of mourning their unexpected charm. Suddenly, in this country where health and happiness are guaranteed by increasingly modern methods, you discover that men die. . . . The cemeteries remind you that each existence is unique and each man an absolute. . . . In America the tombs assert with the greatest authority that man is still human. . . . Their cemeteries have more personality than their cities. Among these slabs half-sunk into the ground, one can escape at last from the banality of everyday life.

L'Amérique au jour le jour [1]

If he told me one day to meet him exactly twenty-two months later on the Acropolis, at five o'clock in the afternoon, I could be sure of finding him there then, punctual to the minute. In a more general way I knew that no harm could ever come to me from him—unless he were to die before I died.

The Prime of Life [2]

I hung up, but my mind was not at ease; this warning had a completely different meaning from the one in 1940; then, it had been external dangers that were threatening Sartre; suddenly I realized that, like everyone else, he was carrying his own death within him. It was something I had never faced up to; to counter it, I invoked my own disappearance from the world, which though it filled me with terror, also reassured me; but at that moment I wasn't involved: what did it matter whether or not I was on earth the day he disappeared from it? What did it matter whether I survived him or not?—that day would still come. In twenty years, tomorrow, the threat was still the same: he was going to die. A black enlightenment! Sartre recovered. But something irrevocable had happened; death had closed its hand around me; it was no longer a metaphysical scandal, it was a quality of our arteries; it was no longer a sheath of night around us, it was an intimate presence penetrating my life, changing the taste of things, the quality of the light, my memories, the things I wanted to do: everything.

The Force of Circumstance [3]

Tuesday 14 October. These really are days of horror. It was like this in the plane that had lost an engine six hours out of Shannon: constant fear, with brief respites followed by a fresh onslaught of fear. It's the same with Sartre. Now and then he seems better; then, like [*sic*] yesterday, he stumbles over words, has difficulty walking, his handwriting and his spelling are appalling, and I am appalled. The left ventricle is tired, the doctor says. He needs a real rest, which is just what he won't take. Our death is inside us, but not like the stone in the fruit, like the meaning of our life; inside us, but a stranger to us, an enemy, a thing of fear. Nothing else counts. My book, the criticisms, the letters I get, the people who talk to me about it, everything that would otherwise have given me pleasure, rendered utterly void. I haven't even the strength to go on with this diary. . . . I think I'm going to stop keeping this diary. . . . I put the pages in a folder, and wrote on it, impulsively: Diary of a defeat. And I never touched it again. . . . A little while later, chatting with Herbaud, a very old friend, I said that, basically, there was nothing else for us to look forward to except our own death or the deaths of those close to us. Who'll go first? Who'll see the others out? Those were the questions I was asking now when I thought about the future. "Now, now," he said to me, "we haven't reached that stage yet; you've always been too old for your years." And yet, I wasn't wrong. . . .

Ibid. [4]

The only thing that can happen now at the same time new and important is misfortune. Either I shall see Sartre dead, or I shall die before him. It is appalling not to be there to console someone for the pain you cause by leaving him. It is appalling that he should abandon you and then not speak to you again. Unless I am blessed by a most improbable piece of good fortune, one of these fates is to be mine. Sometimes I want to finish it all quickly so as to shorten the dread of waiting.

Ibid.[5]

But we found Nizan most intriguing when he approached anywhere near his pet obsession, the idea of death. Though he never openly alluded to the fact, we knew how anguished a state he could get into at the thought of one day vanishing for all eternity: he would trail round for days on end from one cheap bar to the next, drinking glass after glass of cheap red wine to keep this terrifying prospect at bay. He had asked himself whether the Socialist creed might not somehow help him to exorcise it, and felt quite optimistic as to prospects; but his lengthy interrogation of young Russian Communists concerning this topic had elicited a unanimous reply—in the face of death, comradeship and solidarity were no help at all, and they were all scared of death themselves. Officially—as, for instance, when he was reporting on his trip abroad at some meeting—Nizan interpreted facts in an optimistic way. To the extent that progress was made in solving technical problems he explained, love and death would regain their former importance in the U.S.S.R.: a new humanism was being born. But in private conversation with us he spoke very differently. It had been a great blow to him to discover that, in Russia as in France, the individual was alone when he died, and knew it.

The Prime of Life [6]

Nizan had been killed. Where, and the precise circumstances of his death, remained uncertain, but there was no doubt that he *was* dead. His wife and children had fled to America. My heart turned over at the news. Had Nizan, who so loathed the very thought of death, foreseen his own demise?

Ibid.[7]

She [Hélène] was never to see our father again, since he died that July. He had been operated on for prostate trouble, and at first he was thought to have made a good recovery. But months of undernourishment had weakened him, and the defeat and subsequent occupation had given him a grievous shock, so that the onset of senile tuberculosis carried him off in a few days. He faced death with an indifference that amazed me, though he had often said it mattered little to him whether he died on one day rather than another, since death was in any case inevitable. Besides, he had little in common with this new world of ours, and very few reasons for continuing to stay alive in it. He did not struggle: I was amazed at the peaceful way he returned to nothingness. He had no illusions, either: he asked me if I could, without causing my mother distress, see to it that no priest attended his deathbed. (She did, in fact, conform to this wish of his.) I sat with him through his last moments, and watched the grim, protracted struggle with which life finally extinguishes itself, vainly trying to grasp the mystery of this departure to no destination. I stayed a long while alone with him when he had breathed his last: at first, though dead, he was still there, it was my father, but then he receded dizzily from me as I watched, and I found myself bent over a mere corpse.

Ibid.[8]

Jouvet took no part in these debates. For all practical purposes he was already dead; his heart was bad, he knew he was more or less doomed, and on Ash Wednesday he'd had himself photographed receiving the Ashes. He loathed Sartre's blasphemies. His right thumb riveted to his left pulse, his eye on his watch, he pretended to be timing the scenes but in fact let them run through without making a single observation.

Force of Circumstance [9]

For years I had been having my work typed by Lucienne Baudin, a very pleasant woman my own age; she had a little daughter, about ten years old. Despite several affairs with men, her tastes were more inclined toward liaisons with other women; she lived with a woman in her fifties; they brought the child up together. She used to tell me about her problems, her financial difficulties, her friendships, her love affairs, and the whole lesbian world, so much less well known than the world of the male homosexual. I didn't see her often, but I always got on well with her when I did. After a certain length of time she began to do her work very badly and unpunctually; she became nervous. "I think

I've got something wrong with one of my breasts," she told me. I urged her to see a doctor. "I can't stop working." A year later, she told me: "I've got a cancer; it's already the size of a nut." She was sent to the Cancer Institute at Villejuif; I went to visit her, and when I walked in she burst into tears; she was sharing a room with three other patients; one of them, who had just had a breast removed, kept shrieking with pain between her morphine injections; one of the others had had her right breast removed a few years earlier, and now the left one was infected. Lucienne was reduced to a state of terror. It was too late to operate and they were treating her with radiation. The treatment was not successful. They sent her home and injected her with male hormones. When I went to see her again I could scarcely recognize her; her face was swollen, an incipient moustache darkened her upper lip and she spoke in a man's voice; the only thing that was still the same was the shining whiteness of her teeth. Every now and then she would put her hand to her bandaged breast and groan. I sensed how fragile and painful that bundle of decaying glands was, and felt like running away. She cried. She had written to faith healers, had tried miracle drugs, and dreamed of getting to America to consult specialists. And she cried. They took her to the hospital. In the beds on either side, old women were dying of cancer. They went on with the hormone injections. Puffed up like a balloon, bearded, grotesquely hideous, she went on suffering, unresigned to death. When I came back from Saint-Tropez, her friend told me that she was dying; the next day she was dead, after fighting for twenty-four hours. "She looks like a woman of eighty," her friend told me. I hadn't the courage to go and see her corpse.

Ibid.[10]

I greeted the Pope's death with a certain amount of pleasure, as well as that of John Foster Dulles.

Ibid.[11]

Shortly after that—exactly ten years after the doctors had told him: "You've got another ten years"—Boris Vian died of anger and a heart attack during a private screening of his film *I'll Spit on Your Graves*. I learned the news one afternoon when I arrived at Sartre's and picked up *Le Monde*. I had seen him for the last time at Les Trois Baudets. We'd taken a drink together; he had scarcely changed since the first time we talked. I had been very fond of him. Yet it was only several days later, coming across a picture in *Match* of a bier covered with a piece of cloth, that I realized: it's Vian under there. And I understood that if nothing in me revolted at that, it was because I was already used to the idea of my own death.

Ibid.[12]

I was alone in Sartre's apartment one January afternoon when the telephone rang. "Camus has just been killed in a car crash," Lanzmann told me. He was coming back from the south of France with a friend, the car had smashed into a plane tree, and he was killed instantly. I put down the receiver, my throat tight, my lips trembling. "I'm not going to start crying," I said to myself, "he didn't mean anything to me anymore." I stood there, leaning against the window, watching night come down over Saint-Germain-des-Prés, incapable of calming myself or of giving way to real grief. Sartre was upset as well, and we spent the whole evening with Bost talking about Camus. Before getting to bed I swallowed some belladénal pills; I hadn't taken any since Sartre's recovery, I ought to have gone to sleep; I remained completely wide awake. I got up, threw on the first clothes I found, and set out walking through the night. It wasn't the fifty-year-old man who'd just died I was mourning; not that just man without justice, so arrogant and touchy behind his stern mask, who had been struck out of my heart when he gave his approval to the crimes of France; it was the companion of our hopeful years, whose open face laughed and smiled so easily, the young, ambitious writer, wild to enjoy life, its pleasures, its triumphs, and comradeship, friendship, love and happiness. Death had brought him back to life; for him time no longer existed, yesterday had no more truth now than the day before; Camus as I had loved him emerged from the night about me, in the same instant recovered and painfully lost. Every time a man dies, a child dies too, and an adolescent and a young man as well; everyone weeps for the one who was dear to him. A fine, cold rain was falling; along the Avenue d'Orléans, there were bums sleeping in the doorways, hunched up in another world. Everything tore at my heart: this poverty, this unhappiness, this city, the world and life, and death.

When I woke up, I thought: He can't see this morning. It wasn't the first time I'd said that to myself; but every time is the first time. Cayatte came over, I remember, and we talked about the scenario; the conversation was just a pretence; far from having left the world, Camus, by the violence of the event that had struck him down, had become the centre of it and I could no longer see anything except through his dead eyes. I had gone over to the other side where there is nothing, and realized, with a dumb pain, how everything still continued to exist though I was no longer there; all day I teetered on the edge of that impossible experience: touching the other side of my own non-being.

That evening I had planned to go see *Citizen Kane* again; I got to the theatre too early and sat down in the café opposite, in the Avenue de l'Opéra. There were people reading newspapers, quite indifferent to the big headline on the front page and the photograph that was blinding me. I thought of the woman who loved Camus, of her agony at encountering that face on every street corner, a public face that must seem to belong to everyone else now as much as to her, a face that could no longer speak and tell her it wasn't so. What a refinement of torture, I thought, one's secret despair proclaimed and trumpeted to the wind at every street corner. Michel Gallimard had been badly injured; he used to come to our celebrations in 1944 and 1945; he too died. Vian, Camus, Michel: the series of deaths had begun, it would go on till it reached mine, inevitably too soon, or too late.

Ibid.[13]

At the beginning of the winter, Richard Wright had suddenly succumbed to a heart attack. I had discovered New York with him, I had kept a whole store of precious images of him that were suddenly snatched from me into the void. In Antibes, a telephone call informed me of the death of Merleau-Ponty; in his case, too, quite suddenly, the heart had stopped. This life I'm living isn't mine any more, I thought. Certainly I no longer imagined I could maneuver it the way I wanted, but I still believed I had some contribution to make towards its construction; in fact, I had no control over it at all. I was merely an impotent onlooker watching the play of alien forces: history, time and death. This inevitability did not even leave me the consolation of tears. I had exhausted all my capacities for revolt, for regret, I was vanquished, I let go. Hostile to the society to which I belonged, banished by my age from the future, stripped fibre by fibre of my past, I was reduced to facing each moment with nothing but my naked existence. Oh, the cold!

Ibid.[14]

This already dark autumn turned finally to utter blackness in a drama enacted on the other side of the Atlantic. At the beginning of October Fanon had suffered a relapse and his friends had sent him to the United States for treatment; despite his repugnance, he had accepted. He had stopped over in Rome, and Sartre spent a few hours in his hotel room along with Boulahrouf, the G.P.R.A. representative in Italy. Fanon lay flat on his bed, so exhausted that he didn't open his mouth during the whole interview; his face tense, he kept shifting his position the whole time the only way he could express his revolt against the passivity to which his body had been reduced.

On my return to Paris, Lanzmann had shown me some letters and cables from Fanon's wife. As a member of the G.P.R.A., Fanon had supposed that he would be warmly welcomed in Washington; he had been left to rot in his hotel room for ten days, alone and without medical attention. She had gone over to join him with their six-year-old son. Finally admitted to a hopsital, Fanon had just been operated on; they had changed all his blood, in the hope that the shock to his system would start his marrow functioning again, but there was no hope of recovery; at the most, he would live another year. She wrote again, she telephoned; at a distance of 4,000 miles we followed his death agony day by day. Fanon's book came out, there were articles loading him with praise; his wife read him the ones in *L'Express* and *L'Observateur.* "That's not going to get me my marrow back," he said. One night, at about two, she telephoned through to Lanzmann: "Franz is dead." He had caught double pneumonia. Beneath the restrained tone of her letters, one could detect her real despair, and Lanzmann, though not knowing her very well, flew over to Washington. He returned after a few days, appalled and shaken. Fanon had lived every moment of his death and savagely refused to accept it; his aggressive sensitivity had cast off all restraint in his deathbed fantasies; he loathed the Americans, all racists in his eyes, and distrusted the entire hospital staff; the last morning, as he woke up, he betrayed obsessions by saying to his wife: "Last night they put me in the washing machine . . ." His son had gone into his room one day when they were giving him a transfusion; he was lying there with tubes connecting him to a series of plastic bags, some full of red corpuscles, some of white corpuscles and blood platelets; the child rushed out screaming: "The bad men have cut Daddy up with knives!" He went through the streets of Washington waving the green and white flag defiantly.

The Algerians sent a special airplane to take Fanon's body back to Tunis. He was buried in an A.L.N. cemetery; for the first time, and in the middle of the war, the Algerians gave one of their people a national funeral. For a week or two I kept seeing Fanon's photograph all over the place in Paris: in the kiosks on the cover of *Jeune Afrique*, in the window of the Maspero bookstore, younger, calmer than I had ever seen him, and very handsome. His death lay heavy on us because he had weighted it with all the intensity of his life.

Ibid.[15]

Suddenly, hell was back on earth. Marie-Claude Radziewski had given him a file which contained accounts of the treatment inflicted by the *harkis*, in the cellars of the Goutte d'Or, on Moslems handed over to them by the D.S.T.: electrodes, burning, impaling on bottles, hangings, stranglings. The physical tortures were interspersed with psychological treatments. Lanzmann wrote an article on the subject for *Les Temps Modernes* and published the dossier of complaints. A girl student told me that she had been in the street near the Goutte d'Or and seen bleeding men being dragged from one house to another by the *harkis*. The people living in the neighborhood heard screams every night. "Why? Why? Why?" The unendingly repeated cry of a fifteen-year-old Algerian boy who had watched his whole family being tortured * kept tearing at my eardrums and my throat. Oh, how mild they had been in comparison, those abstract storms of revolt I had once felt against the human condition and the idea of death! One can engage in convulsive struggles against fatality, but it discourages anger. And at least my horror had been directed at something outside myself. Now, I had become an object of horror in my own eyes. Why? Why? Why must I wake up every morning filled with pain and rage, infected to the very marrow of my bones with a disease I could neither accept nor exorcise? Old age is, in any case, an ordeal, the least deserved, according to Kant, and the most unexpected according to Trotsky; but I could not bear its driving the existence which until then had contented me into this abyss of shame. "My old age is being made a living horror!" I told myself. And when there is no pride left in life, death becomes even more unacceptable; I never stopped thinking about

* Reported by Benoît Rey in an excellent and appalling book: *Les Egorgeurs.*

it now: about mine, about Sartre's. Opening my eyes each morning, I would say to myself: "We're going to die." And: "Life is a
hell." I had nightmares every night. There was one that came
quite often, and I noted down one version of it.

Last night, a dream of extreme violence. I am with Sartre in this
studio; the phonograph is motionless beneath its cloth cover. Suddenly, music, without my having moved. There is a record on the
turntable, it revolves. I twist the control to stop it; impossible to do
so, it turns faster and faster, the needle can't keep up, the tone arm
gets into the most amazing positions, the inside of the phonograph
is roaring like a furnace, there seem to be flames, and the black surface of the record is becoming insanely shiny. At first, the notion
that the phonograph is going to collapse under the strain, mild panic
which then becomes all-devouring: *Everything* is going to explode; a
supernatural rebellion, incomprehensible, the collapse of all that exists.
I am afraid, I am at the end of my rope; I think of calling a specialist.
I seem to think he's been here, but then I'm the one who thought of
disconnecting the phonograph, and I was afraid when I touched the
plug; it stopped. What a mess! The tone arm reduced to a twisted
little stick, the needle in shreds, the record shattered, the turntable
already ruined, the accessories blasted out of existence, and the disease
still lurking inside the machine.

At the moment when I awoke and went back over it in my
mind, this dream seemed to me to have an obvious meaning: the
mysterious and untamable force was that of time and circumstance, it was laying waste my body (that pitiful, blasted twig
that had once been an arm), it was hacking away, threatening
my past, my life, all that makes me what I am, with total destruction.

Ibid.[16]

Essentially and existentially many of the essays involve the
problem of death; the death of others, however, is conspicuously
absent in these. In *L'Amérique au jour le jour*, because "People
don't speak easily about death in America," Simone de Beauvoir
denigrates the Americans for their evasion of death and speaks in
enthusiastic terms about American cemeteries. Whereas the gen-
eralization that prompts this development and others like it is
valid: "One of the most striking characteristics is the degree to
which they refuse to ask fundamental questions about the world

and themselves" [17] (and she will say the same thing about women writers at the end of *Le Deuxième Sexe*) the particular development on the charm of the cemeteries seems somewhat gratuitous. Is "the reality of death" revealed in "these gardens of mourning" any more than in "the pleasant funeral parlors situated between a drugstore and a bar"? Statements like "Suddenly . . . you discover that men die. . . . The cemeteries remind you that each existence is unique and each man an absolute" suggest that the death of others is as far removed from the daily life of the writer as of the people she is writing about. The death of others comes, during the hectic fete of the voyage and notations on the voyage, as a momentary and unpleasant intrusion which a few banal formulae make inoffensive. The death of others is present in America, as elsewhere, on all human faces. It depends on who is looking. The most significant aspect of this passage is that Simone de Beauvoir did not see it. Again her criticism tells us less about America than it does about Simone de Beauvoir.

In the last two volumes of the memoirs she is obliged to see because those who die are members of her immediate entourage. Simone de Beauvoir's indifference to the death of those whom she does not know is counterbalanced by her anguish at most, not all, of the deaths of those she knows. This anguish reaches its greatest intensity in the projected death of Jean-Paul Sartre.

Very early in their relationship, Simone de Beauvoir's absolute dependency on Sartre's presence is revealed in the terror of "unless he were to die before I died." This terror which is always close to the surface of her consciousness completely overwhelms her whenever Sartre is seriously ill. It is the only obsession that seems as strong as the obsession with her own inevitable nothingness.

In the first quotation from *La Force de l'âge* another aspect of her relationship to him underlines the Godlike role he plays in her life, her complete faith in his word. From 1929 on, because Sartre exists, the three theological virtues, faith, hope, and charity, are reinstated outside the church. It is interesting to speculate on what Simone de Beauvoir would have become had she not encountered a man endowed with the exceedingly rare qualities of Jean-Paul Sartre, or rather what or whom she would have turned to for strength, solace, and belief. He is her rock and shield; therefore he is also her screen. From the age of twenty-one Simone de Beauvoir has never really stood alone. The same general criticism which she applies to women at the end of *Le Deuxième Sexe* may well be applied to her: "What woman needs first of all is to undertake, in anguish and pride, her apprenticeship in abandonment and transcendence." [18] In the bleakest moments Sartre is reassuringly present, and his presence guarantees order and reassures. Sartre is Simone de Beauvoir's most efficacious means of evasion. The intensity of her anguish concerning his specific death prevents her from coming to terms with the idea of death. It is, so to speak, caught on Sartre.

The second quotation that deals with Sartre's death reveals the same intensity and a naïveté that can only be explained by excessive egotism. There was every reason to be alarmed at the fact that Sartre was suddenly hospitalized because of high blood-pressure during a trip to Moscow. But what follows is curious: "Suddenly, I realized that, like everyone else, he was carrying his own death within him. It was something I had never faced up to." Unless there is an extreme situation, unless she is forced to confront certain realities, she evades them or does not see them. This means that her mode of reaction is hysterical, since the awareness is always so sudden, the situation so critical. The real problem is that Simone de Beauvoir cannot sustain this awareness and that much of the time she does not know, or feel, that men are indeed mortal.

The paradoxical nature of her dependency on Sartre is quite clear. On the one hand he gives her strength, but on the other he undermines the walls he constructs because he will one day die. Were it not for Sartre, Simone de Beauvoir might have been obliged to "undertake in anguish and pride, her apprenticeship in abandonment and transcendence"; but, after the death of Zaza, were it not for Sartre she might never have been capable of feeling as strongly about another human being. Sartre's mortality, when she confronts it, brings her to the edge of a real encounter with death and provides some of the most intensely poetic moments in the memoirs.

The third and longest episode that involves Sartre's death is perhaps the apotheosis of anguish in the memoirs. The feeling of anguish is reinforced at the beginning of the episode by the use of the diary and the brevity of the entries. In spite of specific references to Sartre's physical manifestations we have no sense of Sartre's suffering, only of Simone de Beauvoir's. "I am appalled. . . . My book . . . everything that would otherwise have given me pleasure."

The episode terminates in her conversation with André Herbaud, in which old age and death, the death of others and of herself, are seen as the only reality, that is, the only future. Simone de Beauvoir has rediscovered an important truth in these pages, but the truth has come too late for her to cope with it. All she can do is to reiterate her helplessness and the meaninglessness of human activity in face of the inevitable. No attempt is made either to explore the horror or to relate these low, low points to the highest. It is not by chance that the last pages of the memoirs repeat the truth discovered during the period of Sartre's illness: the imminence of death and the emptiness at the heart of all things; the essential failure of every human life. The sentence that best translates all this is the very simple: "Either I shall see Sartre dead, or I shall die before him." This is as close as Simone de Beauvoir ever comes, except for certain passages on the death of her mother, to a sense of reciprocity with another in the confrontation with death. What could have been an important point of departure remains a conclusion.

The other deaths recorded in *La Force de l'âge* and *La Force des choses* reveal a similar pattern, a similar weakness. Whether Simone de Beauvoir is moved, as by the death of Sartre's friend, the writer Paul Nizan, shot at the beginning of the war; the young

poet Bourla, arrested and shot during the Occupation; her secretary Lucienne Baudin, who died of breast cancer; Boris Vian,
who died at thirty-three of a bad heart; Albert Camus, killed in
an automobile accident; Richard Wright and Merleau-Ponty, both
victims of sudden heart attacks; Franz Fanon, who died of leu-
kemia; or whether she is indifferent, as in the death of her father,
the illness of Louis Jouvet; or simply cruel, as in the brief biting
obituary on John Foster Dulles and Pope Pius the Twelfth—the
pattern is clear: someone suffers and dies. Simone de Beauvoir
either goes through a crisis of intense anguish or merely records
the death as another event. In both cases, and despite her unflinch-
ing respect for the least pleasant detail—as in her descriptions of
the suffering of Lucienne Baudin, and Franz Fanon—she forgets.
The experience is always new, not because each death is unique
but because in between deaths she lives in a world of immortals.
The weakness is in the gap between anguish-solitude and elation-
solidarity. It is most blatant when she describes her reactions to
mass demonstrations during the Algerian war. These reactions
explain some of the comments in the Jouvet, Camus, Dulles, and
Pius obituaries. They expose Simone de Beauvoir's most serious
limitation.

The limitation is announced, and one would have thought
exorcised, in the first of the two passages on Paul Nizan and
death. Nizan, haunted by death, hoping that in a socialist world
death would no longer be a solitary, terrifying adventure and
discovering that "in Russia as in France, the individual was alone
when he died, and knew it" is an exemplary model of lucidity.
Yet Simone de Beauvoir from the end of the Second World War
on refuses this model. She commits the same error as did Nizan,
but she never sees the error, and she thrashes around blindly,
either bemoaning her own nothingness or extolling the metaphysical virtues of a politically unified left-wing crowd: "As-
tonished to find itself walking along like this unmolested, the
crowd became infected with tremendous gaiety. And how good
it felt! Solitude is a form of death, and as I felt the warmth of

human contact flow through me again, I came back to life. . . .
It had been a marvelous day and one that encouraged us to
hope." [19] Solitude and anguish have become the products of bourgeois conditioning; collective gaiety the product of left-wing
ideology.

As in the earlier essay, "Oeil pour oeil," a political choice
becomes the most important of all choices, since from it all other
attitudes and values are deduced. Those whose choices differ become mortal enemies. The death of a political adversary is, for
Simone de Beauvoir, an occasion for rejoicing. Thus the policies
of Dulles, the religious affiliation of the Pope, less overtly Jouvet's
Catholicism and Camus' anticommunism are sufficient reason
for an automatic process of exclusion. Jouvet, dying, is presented
as a silly, frightened man because he is Catholic, whereas Fanon,
who was equally frightened, is presented as a courageous victim
because of his political opinions. Under these conditions the
death of another person takes on alarming possibilities. Simone
de Beauvoir's depression, her rage that is almost madness during
the period of the Algerian war, is at times so intense that one
senses the urge to kill, to destroy all opposition, violently, at
once. "Ten thousand Algerians had been herded into the Vel'
d'Hiv, like the Jews at Drancy once before. Again I loathed it
all—this country, myself, the whole world. . . . They could have
blown up the Acropolis then, and Rome, and the whole earth,
and I wouldn't have lifted a finger to stop them." [20] The Acropolis and Rome are, of course, the two outstanding symbols of Western thought and of Christianity. Her own violent reactions become the basis of an apologetics for violence.

A dream which she had during this period and recounts at
length is extremely significant. The dream is preceded by a
description of the information she had received from different
sources on the tortures to which Arabs were being submitted in
Paris itself. Her reaction is more excessive but similar to the one
provoked by previous deaths. It is, as one might expect, completely subjective. She associates the torture with her revolt

against the "human condition and the idea of death" and with the trials of old age. The conclusion at which she arrives has nothing whatever to do with the horror of the Algerian war: "My old age is being made a living horror! . . . 'We're going to die.' . . . 'Life is hell.' . . . I had nightmares every night."

The dream and her interpretation of it reveal the same old anguish about her own death, her own nothingness. Sartre is present, but powerless; he does not act. The frenzy of the phonograph can only be controlled by Simone de Beauvoir. She does finally manage to stop the delirious dance, though not the inner source of the destructive movement. There is no specific reference to the Algerian war. The dream is all about the rhythm and anguish, the will to destruction, of Simone de Beauvoir's world. It would seem then that her political passions are directly related to her untamed fears and that, in part, she used her frenzy about the Algerian war as an outlet for older and deeper wounds. It is the preoccupation with death that she has never adjusted to that makes her a partisan of violence, that propels her to condemn her enemies and to long for their annihilation. To run away from the dread of death is eventually to take the side of death, to become death's accomplice. Political fanaticism is a symptom of a fundamental malady.

Whether Simone de Beauvoir is indifferent or committed, the death of others, in peace or in war, in fiction or in real life, is always felt in relation to her protagonist's or her own persistent anguish. The fact that she ages is more important in determining her attitudes than anything that happens to anyone else, including Sartre, or than any event that takes place in the world. As she ages the obsession grows, and the evasions, particularly in their political form, become more grotesque. The death of others reinforces the original intuition of nothingness. From the old jacket to deaths in fiction and autobiography there has been no important change either in the anguish or in the means of coping with it. Simone de Beauvoir's encounters with death have been encounters with her own death. The bell tolls always and only for her.

CHAPTER IX

The Death of Mother

The death of Simone de Beauvoir's mother is the most detailed of all the encounters with death. It is the only death to which an entire book is devoted although it might be said that the memoirs are, in fact, about the death of Simone de Beauvoir. This book, in which there is more mother and less I, is perhaps Simone de Beauvoir's best. Neither fiction nor memoir, *Une Mort très douce* is a *récit-reportage* shorter in length and more tightly constructed than Simone de Beauvoir's other writings. The reader follows the thirty or more days of the intestinal cancer's final evolution, the thirty or more days of modern medicine's attempts to preserve lingering life, the thirty or more days of two sisters in their mid-fifties watching their seventy-eight-year-old mother die, the last days of a woman who does not want to die.

The death of a mother is always a very special death. Psychoanalytic evidence and hypothesis have accustomed us to recognize the complex feelings of desire, guilt, and horror that a mother's death arouses in a child—of any age. Modern literature has both suggested and confirmed psychoanalytic theory with abundant examples. The death of the mother is a crucial event that determines attitudes and behavior and that brings the "child" to an anguished awareness of human precariousness and solitude. In the case of Simone de Beauvoir there is no fictional transposition, although there is, of course, the essential distance between an experience that does and does not exist in words. Once the story is written down it makes little difference whether it was invented by the author or lived through and told. In both cases the facts which we confront are verbal.

The reader who is familiar with the three volumes of Simone de Beauvoir's memoirs is familiar, too, with the figure of Françoise de Beauvoir. Simone de Beauvoir portrays her mother as a rather attractive but silly woman, a willing victim of the Catholic milieu to which she belonged and enthusiastically adhered. The reader shares Simone de Beauvoir's resentment of the innumerable prejudices that clogged Françoise de Beauvoir's mind and heart and that restricted her capacity to feel and to see. Simone de Beauvoir is quite explicit about her own preference for her nonconformist father. She was never very close to her mother, and one senses that her revolt against the despicable bourgeoisie is, in part, an outgrowth of her revolt against Françoise de Beauvoir. And yet when Georges de Beauvoir, deeply shocked by the defeat of France and the Occupation, died quietly in July 1941, Simone de Beauvoir was but little affected; her father's indifference to *his* death may be largely responsible for her indifference to it. Her mother was not indifferent to her death and neither was Simone de Beauvoir. What she thought she felt about her mother does not coincide with what she feels during the long agony.

The pity, horror, and helplessness the reader of *Une Mort très douce* feels, corresponds both to the author's central emotion and to the underlying theme. No attempt is made at any moment in the main body of the *récit* to transcend the facts of dying or the sentiments, gestures, and words of the woman who is dying and the daughters who are watching her die. The irony of both the Dylan Thomas quotation which is used as an epigraph, "Do not go gentle into that good night," and of the title is continued throughout the book in a courageous desire to break through some of the simplistic left-wing ideology that often replaces intelligent analysis in her other books. When the bourgeois Catholic images which she had so firmly and so conveniently affixed to her mother are displaced, a human being begins to die, and Simone de Beauvoir begins to suffer for someone other than herself. Sartre is absent from all but two scenes in the *récit*, and this significant absence helps to explain Simone de Beauvoir's ability to sustain, for so long a time, an excruciating lucidity. Is it that she has nothing and no one to turn to for solace or as a means of evasion? Is it perhaps that this time none of the usual havens are sufficient because reality is so blatant?

Une Mort très douce is the only one of Simone de Beauvoir's books in which the hectic rhythm which she projects on the world is abruptly interrupted and the interruption prolonged. There is an outlandish contrast between the joyful scenes of mass demonstrations in the preceding volume, *La Force des choses*, the frenetic tempo of Simone de Beauvoir's voyages alluded to in the opening pages of *Une Mort très douce*, and the scene of the hospital bed on which Françoise de Beauvoir lies. The image of a human being agonizing on a bed which Simone de Beauvoir has been avoiding since *L'Invitée* and which is her central obsession is forced upon her by the event.

Before the fall that disclosed her mother's cancer, Simone de Beauvoir was a faithful but inattentive daughter. Between trips to Rome, Prague, and elsewhere she would visit her mother for a few hours. Their relationship was affectionate but distant.

The quotations that follow reveal the manner in which this encounter acts upon Simone de Beauvoir's usual defenses, how they crumble, and which ones, nevertheless, remain intact.

I was not much affected. In spite of her frailty my mother was tough. And after all, she was of an age to die.[1]

Simone de Beauvoir's first reaction to the dangers of three months in bed for an elderly woman who has apparently broken her pelvic bone is straightforward and abstract. She felt that her mother was basically strong and in no mortal danger—she could not feel her mother as mortal. This reaction was inaccurate; Françoise de Beauvoir was far from "tough." She had an intestinal cancer whose signs—pallor, odor, loss of weight—were detected by friends and completely unsuspected by Simone de Beauvoir and the blundering doctors.

At the same time that she felt that her mother was not going to die, Simone de Beauvoir felt that seventy-eight was after all a proper age for death. It is a well-known cliché that the death of a young person is tragic but that the death of an older person is in the natural order of the biological world and is therefore acceptable. Simone de Beauvoir never uses this cliché when she imagines her own death or Sartre's. Her use of it in connection with her mother reveals a lack of imagination for the suffering of others, a refusal to feel the world as another feels it.

Thirteen pages later, Simone de Beauvoir realizes the vacuity of her own words: "When I said to myself, 'She is of an age to die,' the words were devoid of meaning, as so many words are. For the first time I saw her as a dead body under suspended sentence." [2] What is curious is that it should take so many years and an old body on a hospital bed before Simone de Beauvoir can recognize that her mother is mortal, before she can think the corpse behind the body.

I pictured her distress. She believed in heaven, but in spite of her age, her feebleness, and her poor health, she clung ferociously to this world, and she had an animal dread of death.[3]

Only a few pages separate the second quotation from the first, yet the difference between them is impressive. The story, which Françoise de Beauvoir tells over and over again, of how she fell in her bathroom and crawled for two hours before reaching the telephone, has an immediate and painful impact on Simone de Beauvoir and consequently on the reader. The image of the old woman on all fours seeking help is an image that symbolizes our

apprehension of solitude and old age, of pathetic animal helplessness. It is difficult not to identify with this image. When Simone
de Beauvoir writes "I pictured her distress," she is describing
what is for most people a fairly routine mechanism and what is,
for her, a rare occurrence: the possibility of imagining what it is
like to be someone else, to see and feel differently.

On the first page of the *récit* Simone de Beauvoir writes: "I
was putting papers away when the telephone rang. It was Bost
calling me from Paris: 'Your mother has had an accident,' he said.
I thought: she has been knocked down by a car; she was climbing
laboriously from the roadway to the pavement, leaning on her
stick, and a car knocked her down." [4] Simone de Beauvoir's immediate reaction suggests that she was prepared for some accident to befall her mother. She sees her mother as a lonely, piti-
able victim. She thinks in concrete terms; the car, the sidewalk,
the street, the cane. Her anxiety about her mother, whatever she
may say to the contrary, antedates her mother's fall and the
diagnosis of her illness. This anxiety, composed essentially of
anticipation and guilt, is disclosed in the repetition of "she has
been knocked down by a car. . . . A car knocked her down."
Simone de Beauvoir had for some time thought about how it
would come. Still "I thought" is not nearly as strong as "I pictured her distress." The second verb goes beyond obsession to
identification and compassion. What Simone de Beauvoir is able
to identify with is the "animal dread" of death. This is stronger
than the barriers erected between them by her mother's religious
beliefs and the difference of generation. From the moment that
Simone de Beauvoir realizes that her mother does not want to
die and is afraid of dying, Françoise de Beauvoir is transformed
from a prig and a bigot into a suffering human being.

It was a lovely autumn day with a blue sky: I made my way
through a lead-coloured world, and I realized that my mother's
accident was affecting me far more than I had thought it would.
I could not really see why. It had wrenched her out of the frame-

work, the role, the set of images in which I had imprisoned her:
I recognized her in this patient in bed, but I did not recognize
either the pity or the kind of disturbance that she aroused in me.
. . . I bristled when the privileged classes spoke through my
mother's mouth; but I felt wholly on the side of the bedfast in-
valid struggling to thrust back paralysis and death.[5]

This is the first and only time in the writings of Simone de
Beauvoir that a feeling of solidarity exists for another human
being who is neither a part of a mass (as in the mass demonstra-
tion) nor Jean-Paul Sartre. The information divulged here is crucial to our understanding why: "my mother's accident was affecting me far more than I had thought it would." A particular accident had been foreseen. What was not foreseen was the degree
to which Simone de Beauvoir would react to it. The essential
revelation in this passage is not the revelation of another Françoise de Beauvoir, but the disturbing revelation of another
Simone. It is she who is "wrenched out of the framework, the
role, the set of images in which I had imprisoned her" and what
appears, troubling and unforeseen, is "the pity . . . the kind of
disturbance." "Disturbance" and disorder are what Simone de
Beauvoir has always ferociously tried to avoid. The very words
"privileged classes" and "wholly on the side of" tell us something
about Simone de Beauvoir's philosophical, ideological orientation.
On the side of Satan is the evil elite, including Françoise de Beauvoir. On the side of God, the good oppressed and the good
authentic lucid beings, including Simone de Beauvoir. This version of the human world is not altered by the "pity" and the
"disturbance." Instead, Françoise de Beauvoir's dying is shifted
from Satan's camp to God's. The verb "struggling" makes of
Simone de Beauvoir's mother an agonizing, oppressed victim.
She is saved. The problem now is how Simone de Beauvoir will
cope with her own unexpected reactions that have awakened the
old anguish concerning nothingness and death.

Between the passages already quoted and those that follow an
important fact is disclosed in the book. Françoise de Beauvoir's

illness was finally diagnosed; she had an intestinal cancer and was dying. We learn, too, that Françoise de Beauvoir had for a long time been fearful that she herself would one day have a cancer.

The diagnosis brings to the hospital and to the bedside of Françoise de Beauvoir her younger married daughter Hélène, or Poupette, to whom *Une Mort très douce* is dedicated. Simone de Beauvoir's initial solitude is thus broken by the presence of her sister, who, closer to their mother, now bears a major part of the waiting and watching. Poupette's first words when she arrives at the hospital establish a significant difference between the two sisters:

"But what's the good of tormenting her, if she is dying. Let her die in peace," said Poupette, in tears.[6]

More spontaneous, more direct, less encumbered by ideological and intellectual constructions, Hélène, as seen by her elder sister, is also less prone to sudden hysteria.

I went home; I talked to Sartre; we played some Bartok. Suddenly, at eleven, an outburst of tears that almost degenerated into hysteria.

Amazement. When my father died I did not cry at all. I had said to my sister, "It will be the same for Maman." I had understood all my sorrows up until that night; even when they flowed over my head I recognized myself in them. This time my despair escaped from my control: someone other than myself was weeping in me. I talked to Sartre about my mother's mouth as I had seen it that morning and about everything I had interpreted in it: greediness refused, an almost servile humility, hope, distress, loneliness—the loneliness of her death and of her life—that did not want to admit its existence. And he told me that my own mouth was not obeying me any more: I had put Maman's mouth on my own face and in spite of myself, I copied its movements. Her whole person, her whole being, was concentrated there, and compassion wrung my heart.[7]

Like her sister, Simone de Beauvoir also cries. When she does, she is on the verge of hysteria. These crises have been a part of Simone de Beauvoir's behavior pattern since her childhood, so the reader who is familiar with her memoirs is less amazed than Simone de Beauvoir. When all the props (Sartre and Bartok) are useless, and the situation is extremely painful, Simone de Beauvoir falls apart. That is her way of dealing with the most distressing encounters.

The reader's wonder is at her reiterated naïveté and arrogance: "it will be the same for Maman." This mania for planning and plotting emotional reactions in advance can only be a sign of fear, the fear that if there is no organized plan there will be no means of controlling her emotions and that she will be subject to the dreaded "hysteria," drowned by sorrows, her heart wrung with compassion. Simone de Beauvoir's insistence that before this she has always understood her most severe crises does not convince anyone who has read her memoirs. These past crises seem intimately related to the one provoked by her dying mother, which is easier to understand because of the circumstances— a mother, a hospital, cancer. Simone de Beauvoir's inability to understand her grief and her despair on this occasion can be attributed to the immense weight of ideological conditioning and prejudice.

It is almost as if Simone de Beauvoir were ashamed to admit consciously both the process of identification and the degree to which she identifies with her mother. She is betrayed by her own mouth. Sartre, here, is not a refuge but a perceptive critic. Indeed, this process of identification has been going on since the opening page of the *récit* that announced the accident. Simone de Beauvoir's resistance to it accounts for much of the work's tension. What Simone de Beauvoir has read into the expression of her mother's mouth and imitates unconsciously is her own unavowed solitude. In becoming her dying mother Simone de Beauvoir has momentarily known compassion. It is a rare and precious state, because we are at the same time ourselves and another. Without leaping we can move naturally from the solitude of every human being to some sense of solidarity. Simone de Beauvoir is too upset to move beyond defeat, solitude, and silence. When she recovers she will not make the move because, with recovery, the old conditioning and prejudices return, and the inevitable tendency to leap with words.

This compassion marks the critical moment of this encounter with death. It is the moment when the emptiness at the heart of all things, which for so long had been hers alone, is finally shared. It is the difference between saying and knowing that all men are mortal. In this awareness sustained is the possibility of a new sensibility.

After this episode, Simone de Beauvoir has several moments of heightened consciousness that again break through the protective façade. During a period of relative calm in her mother's agony, Simone de Beauvoir flies to Prague with Sartre. A telegram and a painful telephone call from her sister precipitate her return to Paris. ("I held Maman's hand all the time and she kept begging me not to let her go. She said, 'I shall not see Simone again.'")

I asked the porter to reserve me a place in the aeroplane that was leaving the next morning at half past ten. Engagements had been fixed; Sartre advised me to wait a day or two. Impossible. I did not particularly want to see Maman again before her death; but I could not bear the idea that she should not see me again. Why attribute such importance to a moment since there would be no memory? There would not be any atonement either. For myself I understood, to the innermost fiber of my being, that the absolute could be enclosed within the last moments of a dying person.[8]

Sartre's advice is useless. He is evidently outside the drama and his comments on it are irrelevant. The "porter," the aeroplane," the "engagements" form an appropriate contrast to Hélène de

Beauvoir's laconic account of her mother's condition. They belong to the world of the committed intellectual busily travelling, conferring, lecturing, writing, saving souls, and solving problems which take precedence over the annoying intrusion of death. Simone de Beauvoir's reaction is immediate and simple. Her need to justify it takes us back to the image she has of who she is, or should be, and how she should behave, her suspicion of her own motive, her apparent distrust of spontaneity. The self-consciousness surrounds a decision that is based on doing something to please someone else, particularly her mother, and reveals how much she has to struggle to reach the most evident and simplest conclusions. She finds, in this case, a rather pompous formula: "I understood . . . that the absolute could be enclosed within the last moments of a dying person." She does fight through and she does manage to juggle with an apparent paradox that opposes logic and feeling. But is the word "absolute" which she struggles against using and finally uses really the proper word? The central fact in this paragraph is "I could not bear . . . to the innermost fibre of my being." This is another way of saying that Simone de Beauvoir was drowned by sorrows, her heart wrung with compassion. The danger is that the haughty maxim about the "last moments of a dying person" will usurp the place that rightfully belong to the direct and moving words: "She said: 'I shall not see Simone again.' "

Simone de Beauvoir returns to Paris and finds that her mother has moved closer to death.

My real life took place at her side, and it had only one aim—protecting her. . . . What tried us more than anything were Maman's death-agonies, her resurrections, and our own inconsistency. In this race between pain and death we most earnestly hoped that death would come first. Yet when Maman was asleep with her face lifeless, we would anxiously gaze at the white bed-jacket to catch the faint movement of the black ribbon that held her watch: dread of the last spasm gripped us by the throat.[9]

Never, as companion to Sartre, or mistress or passionate friend, did Simone de Beauvoir allow herself to be caught in a situation in which someone else was so dependent on her. Never, in the brief accounts in the memoirs of those she loved do we sense the tenderness of "protecting her" and the repetition of "maman." There is no sentimentality here, only an extreme human compassion which moves the reader more profoundly than her ponderous maxims. The situation described is located at the limit of human endurance: wishing for death to end suffering and dreading death above all else; seeing the appeal in the eyes of the dying who want neither to suffer nor to die and knowing the inevitability of their suffering and their death. However different dying may be in fact from our imaginings about it, watching someone die who is suffering is worse than our worst fantasies. "Nothing on earth could possibly justify these moments of pointless torment." [10] This Simone de Beauvoir has been able to express.

"The only comfort I have," she [Poupette] said, "is that it will happen to me too. Otherwise it would be too unfair." Yes. We were taking part in the dress rehearsal for our own burial. The misfortune is that although everyone must come to this, each experiences the adventure in solitude. We never left Maman during those last days which she confused with convalescence and yet we were profoundly separated from her. [11]

Hélène's words go further in their implications than her sister's comments on them would suggest. Hélène is saying what she has learned from the experience, a sense of communion with her mother through mortality, whereas Simone de Beauvoir is repeating an eternal verity, "each experiences the adventure in solitude." She finds evidence for this in the fact that her mother was not told that she was dying of cancer, whereas those who watched her die knew. Yet many things in Françoise de Beauvoir's behavior suggest that she did know—not that she had terminal cancer but that she was indeed dying. There are, in this kind of situation, different ways of knowing. The importance of this encounter with death, as Hélène seems to have understood, is that a deep awareness of mortality tends to violate the law of solitude. Again Simone de Beauvoir is separated from her experiences by the language she uses. Language is perhaps the most efficacious instrument of evasion.

Sometimes, though very rarely, it happens that love, friendship, or comradely feeling overcomes the loneliness of death: in spite of appearances, even when I was holding Maman's hand, I was not with her—I was lying to her. Because she had always been deceived, gulled, I found this ultimate deception revolting. I was making myself an accomplice of that fate which was so misusing her. Yet at the same time in every cell of my body I joined in her refusal, in her rebellion: and it was also because of that that her defeat overwhelmed me. Although I was not with Maman when she died, and although I had been with three people when they were actually dying, it was when I was at her bedside that I saw Death, the Death of the dance of death, with its bantering grin, the Death of fireside tales that knocks on the door, a scythe in its hand, the Death that comes from elsewhere, strange, and inhuman: it had the very face of Maman when she showed her gums in a wide smile of unknowingness.[12]

Simone de Beauvoir begins by making exceptions to the general truth she had enunciated earlier, but she gives us no precise example. What she is doing is setting up ideal situations opposed to the one she has just lived through with her mother. The point seems to be that because her mother was always guilty of "bad faith" there was no possibility of an authentic relationship with her. "I was lying to her" is a curious perversion of what did in fact take place and was witnessed by the reader.

Simone de Beauvoir describes her encounter with her mother's death in these terms because, when she comes to the last part of her *récit*, the summing up, she feels obliged, certain laws of composition oblige her, to draw relevant conclusions and she falls back once again on a language that does not relate to the facts of her experience. It is a language within which the elite that

Françoise de Beauvoir represents must be eternally damned. "I was making myself an accomplice of that fate which was so misusing her" seems to have no relation at all to the preceding events: "accomplice" and "fate" refer to the animistic prescientific world of primitive man. The "fate which was so misusing her [*lui faisait violence*]" was old age and intestinal cancer; Simone de Beauvoir was not and could not have been their accomplice. She sets up images of her mother and herself that obscure the problems. The conclusion does not emanate from the phenomena described but from a hypothesis held prior to the experiment. This hypothesis is based on the positive or negative charge of certain words. "I joined in her refusal, in her rebellion"; but is it possible to use words like "refusal" and "rebellion" to describe the behavior of an old woman afraid of dying and of death?

There is a similar though more subtle abuse of language in the last long sentence of the quotation. The parallels established between certain traditional death themes and the expression on her mother's face are subjective and valid. However, the last word, "unknowingness," is ideologically rather than poetically charged. It goes back to "lying," "deceived," "deception." It does not relate to the death of Françoise de Beauvoir, but to a notion of how an elitist bigot should die.

What has occurred, then, in *Une Mort très douce* is not essentially different from what occurred in the other encounters with death; the encounter is followed by an evasion. Here, the encounter is more direct and more profound. Simone de Beauvoir is involved as she never was before, and yet there is the moment when the exploration of the unknown becomes unbearable and she goes back to what is, after all, her fundamental project as a writer: building an acceptable image of herself. This image gets in the way of serious analysis and in the end is quite useless.

CHAPTER X

The Death of Simone de Beauvoir

Régine's appeal in *Tous les Hommes sont mortels*, "Save me," she said, "Save me from death," echoes throughout the work of Simone de Beauvoir, a long and desperate cry for help.

Simone de Beauvoir does not write in order to triumph over death through immortality; that notion belongs to another and a happier age. She writes to reassure herself that she *is* and to create for herself an image in language that reality persistently denies. Writing is both an evasion and a revolt, a means of avoiding death and a means of refusing it. It is essentially an activity that exorcises the loss of identity that accompanies the dread of death. The particular kind of writing Simone de Beauvoir does is directly related to the reason why she writes. Her writing, whether the generic form be novel, essay, memoirs, *récit*, is primarily documentation. Her entire effort over the past forty years in both published and unpublished material has been to draw a portrait of Simone de Beauvoir. The following quotations from an interview in which Simone de Beauvoir expands on the last lines of *La Force des choses* recapitulate and clarify the problem:

I've always been haunted by the passing of time and by the fact that death keeps closing in on us. For me, the problem of time is linked up with that of death, with the thought that we inevitably draw closer and closer to it, with the horror of decay.

. . . So it's not that I've felt that time breaks things up, but rather the fact that I always take my bearings. I mean the fact that I have so many years behind me, so many ahead of me. I count them.[1]

The link between time and death is the central motif of Western European literature since the French Revolution. The preoccupation with time in the greatest writers of the period is essentially a preoccupation with death. To be conscious of mortality is to be conscious of past, present, and future. The attempt to break through the limits posed by mortality is the attempt to stop or to fix time, in an ecstatic experience or in a metaphor. If one is neither a mystic nor a poet, in the large sense of a creator of images, there remains still another possibility:

When one has an existentialist view of the world, like mine, the paradox of human life is precisely that one tries to *be* and, in the long run, merely exists. It's because of this discrepancy that when you've laid your stake on being—and, in a way you always do when you make plans, even if you actually know that you can't succeed in being—when you turn around and look back on your life, you see that you've simply existed. In other words, life isn't behind you like a solid thing, like the life of a God (as it is conceived, that is, as something impossible). Your life is simply a human life. . . . I think that anyone who had a hard life when he was young won't say in later years that he's been "swindled." . . . I've had what I wanted and, when all is said and done, what one wanted was always something else. . . . There is an emptiness in man and even his achievements have this emptiness.[2]

This sense of emptiness, this impossibility of being (which Simone de Beauvoir carefully suggests is a bourgeois symptom), can be partially overcome by a particular form of activity; the perpetual creation of oneself through words. This creation is intended for others who will reflect the image that the subject cannot give to itself.

I wept over her [Maggie Tulliver in *The Mill on the Floss*]
sorry fate for hours. The others condemned her because she was
superior to them; I resembled her, and thenceforward I saw my
isolation not as a proof of infamy but as a sign of my uniqueness.
I couldn't see myself dying of loneliness. Through the heroine,
I identified myself with the author: one day other adolescents,
another me, would bathe with their tears a novel in which I
would tell my own story.[3]

"My own story" is at the origin of Simone de Beauvoir's vocation and a definition of her entire writing career; a metaphysical exhibitionism, an attempt to expose her being to the widest
possible public. This mania for image-making has detrimental
effects on exploration, analysis, lucidity, and on literary creation
itself. In the preoccupation with the self there is no sense of a
reality, physical or human, that is other than an extension of the
self. The self is unique—"my isolation" and the other whom it
requires as reflector is "another me." The ideal reader is an alter
ego, Simone de Beauvoir contemplating Simone de Beauvoir.
When Simone de Beauvoir is not engaged in telling her own
story, not creating her image and receiving its salutary reflection,
she falls apart.

These crises are ascribed to metaphysical anguish, the intimations of nothingness. That the crises are also psychosomatic and
that they have their highest incidence and most intense manifestations during the periods recorded in the memoirs when Simone
de Beauvoir feels abandoned, there can be little doubt. The word
most often used in relation to the worst of the crises is "stone";
"Suddenly I was becoming a stone and steel was splitting it: that
is hell." [4] "Her body was a stone: she wanted to shriek, but stone
has no voice; nor tears." [5] Why "stone"? We think of a stone as
being impassive, insensible. To compare a human being to a stone
is to suggest something inhuman, a different form of being at a
great distance from our usual psychic disturbances. It is the
notion of distance that is essential. The stone is hard, a thing and

a world in itself with unknown laws. A stone is absolute passivity, the absolute victim. The steel that breaks the stone is an
impersonal, therefore unattackable, torturer.

Not all the crises are this virulent. Two quotations from *La
Force de l'âge* reconfirm the importance of the less virulent
anxiety states and indicate quite explicitly that their importance
was never satisfactorily explored:

> I surrendered to their assault [to remorse and to fear] in
> accordance with the dictates of a rhythmical pattern that has
> governed almost the entire course of my life. I would go weeks
> on end in a state of euphoria; and then for a few hours I would
> be ravaged by a kind of tornado that stripped me bare. To justify
> my condition of despair yet further, I would wallow in an abyss
> compounded of death, nothingness, and infinity. When the sky
> cleared again I could never be certain whether I was waking
> from a nightmare or relapsing into some long sky-blue fantasy,
> a permanent dream world.[6]

> Today I believe that, under the specially privileged condition
> in which I exist, life contains two main truths which we must
> face simultaneously, and between which there is no choice—the
> joy of being, the horror of being no more. At the time I vacil-
> lated between one and the other. It was only for brief moments
> that the second triumphed, but I had a suspicion it might be the
> more valuable of the two.[7]

What eventually gets in the way of any significant exploration
of these states is Sartre and ideology. The two obstacles are really
one. Sartre, in his reactions and his advice throughout the memoirs and through the characters in the novels for whom he is the
principal model, tends to minimize, even to explain away, either
metaphysical anguish or anxiety states; to consider them as barriers to action in and on the world. He did so perhaps out of
impatience with Simone de Beauvoir's ups and downs, perhaps
because he felt that in denigrating these states he would restore
her more quickly to an equilibrium or perhaps because he considered these states as uninteresting, the product of a specifically

bourgeois neurosis. There is a conversation in the *Mandarins* between Anne Dubreuilh and her husband Robert in which the positions of Simone de Beauvoir and Sartre are recorded and which illustrate the major difficulty; the problem is badly posed or posed in such a way that the possible answers can only be evasive and insufficient.

"Things are never as important as they seem; they change, they end, and above all, when all is said and done, everyone dies. That settles everything."

"That's just a way of escaping from problems," Robert said. I cut him off. "Unless it's that problems are a way of escaping the truth. Of course," I added, "when you've decided that it's life that's real, the idea of death seems like escape. But conversely . . ."

Robert shook his head. "There's a difference. The fact of living proves you've chosen to believe in life; if one honestly believes that death alone is real, then one should kill oneself. Actually, though, even suicides don't think that."

"It may be that people go on living simply because they're scatterbrained and cowardly," I said. "It's easier that way. But that doesn't prove anything either."

"First of all, it's important that suicide be difficult," Robert said. "And then continuing to live isn't only continuing to breathe. No one ever succeeds in settling down in complete apathy. You like certain things, you hate others, you become indignant, you admire—all of which implies that you recognize the values of life." He smiled. "I'm not worried. We haven't done with discussing the camps and all the other things. Like myself, like everyone, you feel yourself powerless in face of certain overwhelming facts, so you take refuge in a generalized skepticism. You don't really mean it."

I didn't answer. Tomorrow, of course, I'd begin discussing things again, a lot of things. Did that prove they would stop seeming insignificant to me? And if they did, maybe it would be because I'd be deceiving myself again.[8]

Neither Anne nor the reader is convinced, at the end of this conversation, by Robert's answers to his wife's anguish. The choice is not, as Robert states, between life and death, living and dying, participation and indifference. Indeed, there is no choice, and Robert's comments on suicide are grossly irrelevant. Death does not cease to be the fundamental fact and problem of the human condition merely because one can become passionately involved in human situations. The involvements that precede from our animal needs and possibilities in no way negate the pre-occupation with death. The pressing problem is how to integrate life and death, how to maintain the essential knowledge of death at the moment of participation in human affairs. The feeling of anguish is as real as the need for commitment. Robert has for-mulated a misleading dichotomy. When he says: "you take refuge in a generalized skepticism. You don't really mean it," he is doubly wrong. "A generalized skepticism" is the conclusion and consequence of an intense awareness of the vanity of all things. A preoccupation with death leads inevitably to skepticism. And it is very serious. Neither Robert nor Anne sees as an alternative the possibility of maintaining an extreme skepticism and still caring passionately about the human world. They do not see the alternative of synthesis. What Robert means when he says "You don't really mean it" is that Anne's mood will change, that her anguish, although recurrent, is transitory, that when the anguish goes it will be forgotten. This is indeed what happens. At a party that takes place shortly after the dialogue between Anne and Robert, Anne is incensed by the conversation of those to whom she refers as "the worldly and pseudo-worldly." On the basis of this simple social reaction she accepts Robert's analysis: "Sud-denly, I thought, Robert is right. Indifference doesn't exist. . . . Yes, it was out of weariness, laziness, or shame of my ignorance that I had idiotically pretended the contrary." [9] The phrase "Sud-denly, I thought" reveals a major weakness of the character. An absolute value is given to the feeling of the moment, and on the strength of this feeling or intuition a philosophy of life is spon-taneously generated that excludes any conflicting feeling or intui-tion. It is either anguish or total commitment. The inability to relate to past feelings in the present, the abrupt exclusion of an entire region of sensibility, can only result in a drastic reduction and oversimplification of the human case. Simone de Beauvoir's naïveté is a manifestation of the either-or malady, as is the weightlessness of so many of her moral assertions and those of her characters.

Simone de Beauvoir also experiences severe upheavals when her relationship to Sartre is threatened by the presence of another woman. The pattern is always the same: a sense of inferiority or inadequacy, spasms of jealousy, a deep sense of insecurity, attacks of anguish, the inability to swallow, dizziness, a sense of loss of identity. The manner of combatting these symptoms is also the same: the self is reasserted through writing, the telling of the story.

Literature is born when something in life goes slightly adrift. In order to write—as Blanchot showed so well in the paradoxical case of Aytré—the first essential condition is that *reality should no longer be taken for granted;* only then can one both perceive it, and make others do so. . . . My schemes of work remained futile dreams till the day came when that happiness was threatened, and I rediscovered a certain kind of solitude in anxiety. The unfortunate episode of the trio did much more than supply me with a subject for a novel; it enabled me to deal with it.[10]

When Sartre became infatuated with Simone de Beauvoir's student Olga, he attempted to organize a viable trio that included himself, Simone de Beauvoir, and Olga. For Simone de Beauvoir the anguish caused by this arrangement was almost unbearable. Her anguish led to writing. But what is the nature of this act of writing? Is it a screen that enables her to get temporarily past the anguish? What is the nature of the writing itself? Does it examine the anguish or resolve it? Because the anguish is never fully confronted it returns periodically in precisely the same form.

The experience of the trio as it is described in *La Force de l'âge* and transformed as fiction in *L'Invitée* becomes a vehicle for the creation of an image of Simone de Beauvoir, an image created through the shaping of an event. It is significant that for all the major peripeties of her life we have both fiction and memoirs and that the memoirs follow the fiction. Telling a story is not enough; she must tell *her* story. The story told is at least a certainty that things took place in her life. It raises these things to the level of events; it glorifies and aggrandizes them; it gives them solidity. Because of this, Simone de Beauvoir emerges in her own eyes with the identity she always hoped to have in the eyes of others and which she generously accorded to herself.

Françoise in *L'Invitée* covers over her original anguish by her relationship with Pierre, which despite all attempts at justification in egalitarian terms remains a relationship in which Pierre represents for Françoise the absolute. When this relationship, essential to Françoise's metaphysical and psychological survival, is threatened by the presence of the invited guest, Xavière, and Pierre's evident desire for Xavière, Françoise's anguish is so strong that her only manner of handling it is to kill Xavière. This death gives a definitive end and shape to her jealousy. Her jealousy is now behind her; it can be contemplated and since it has become an object of contemplation it has lost its virulence. The death of Xavière functions in the same way for Françoise as the act of writing *L'Invitée* for Simone de Beauvoir. Jealousy, like all forms of anguish, derives its power from its being within, from its being ambiguous and inaccessible to reason. Simone de Beauvoir turns the anguish provoked by jealousy into a consistent tale through which she is able to evade the same anguish with a clear conscience. Françoise in *L'Invitée* becomes a murderess, Simone de Beauvoir in *La Force de l'âge* becomes a tendentious moralist who uses the trio ostensibly as a means of exploring the validity of her relationship with Sartre, but in fact as a means of reinforcing the "we." Thus the real reminders of the emptiness at the heart of Simone de Beauvoir, of the death of Simone de Beauvoir, are held at bay by jealousy and the act of coping with it in fiction.

The memoirs relate four incidents in which Simone de Beauvoir's own death is a real rather than an imagined possibility: two illnesses and two nearly fatal accidents. Significantly, on those rare occasions when she is closest to death she is also farthest away from anguish. The two illnesses provoke more ambiguous reactions.

The first illness, like the jealousy occasioned by Sartre's infatuation for Olga, is an incident both in the novel, *L'Invitée*, and in the second volume of memoirs, *La Force de l'âge*. The nature of the illness plays an important role in the protagonist's reaction to it. Pneumonia is not cancer of the lung, and, even though the period of convalescence is long, recovery is almost certain. A long illness that is not mortal provides a sudden and total rupture with an active, regulated life. It stops routine action and the thought patterns that accompany it. The body takes over, and the mind, in a sense, is at rest. Something has happened that requires all the mind's energy, and it delights in paying the strictest attention to the smallest, least perceptible bodily functions. The mind has neither the need nor the time to imagine. Death is perhaps never so far away as during this form of illness, in which the mind is absorbed by the body and thrives on its busyness.

In the context of *L'Invitée* Françoise's illness serves a double function: it separates her still further from her past life and it removes her for three weeks from Pierre and allows him to strengthen his ties with Xavière. The agitation and the anguish that characterize Françoise's mode of being before and after her illness are temporarily replaced by a "calm indifference." [11] Illness is a refuge from the difficulty of being and loving. Illness hides the void; it depersonalizes and liberates. "Had she really become just anyone? Was that why she felt so light, released from herself, from her whole escort of suffocating joys and worries? She closed her eyes. Smoothly, the car drove on, and time slipped by." [12]

There is an important difference in the manner in which the

same episode is reported in *La Force de l'âge;* it takes place after, and not during, the intense involvement in the trio. Yet, here, too, the illness is a vacation from the intricacies of Simone de Beauvoir's daily life, a welcome change of rhythm and obsessions. The lesson she draws, and she always draws a lesson, is the same as in *L'Invitée:* "Anything, it was clear, could happen to me, just as it could to any other person. Now here was a revolution." [13] This is the identical surprise that accompanies all her important encounters. This time, however, there is no anguish but rather a pleasure in escaping from herself. There is pleasure because illness, unlike the confrontation with the old jacket, provides a substitute world.

In 1935 Simone de Beauvoir did not realize how ill she really was; this ignorance may have contributed to her calm. In 1952, depressed by personal and intellectual difficulties, she reacted quite differently to the presence of a small lump on her breast. The sequence of events, mental and physical, that compose this episode, has become a familiar pattern in our cancer-oriented society. The first sign of an unusual growth and the oscillation between "It's nothing" and deep uneasiness; the identification with someone who did have cancer, in this case Simone de Beauvoir's secretary Lucienne Baudin, whose grotesque end she had recorded; the confiding in a close friend, in this case Sartre, who was always verbally calm and seemingly unconcerned; the first visit to the doctor, who both reassures her and suggests the worst; the increased anxiety preceding the operation and the continuing consolations of the close friend (Sartre's, to be sure, are far from typical: "if the worst came to the worst, I could count on twelve or so more years of life; twelve years from then the atomic bomb would have disposed of us all").[14] And finally the hospital. Here, there is a radical change. The routine of the hospital neutralizes the anguish and transforms it into a "calm indifference." When Simone de Beauvoir regained consciousness after the operation she was immediately informed that she did not have cancer. Her reaction continues to follow a predictable pattern, but the words used are particularly revealing: "angels came and rocked me to sleep . . . full of wonder at finding myself still whole and delivered from my fear." [15] Before her entrance into the hospital her fear was directed to specific images: "the hairy face of Lucienne Baudin and her agony . . . the removal of the breast . . . the old women in the room with Lucienne; ten years later the other breast becomes infected, one dies in appalling agony." [16]

The fear involves mutilation, suffering and a time limit on life. The relief does not relate to those precise fears but to the entire universe of fear. Simone de Beauvoir has not escaped from cancer but from the torment that accompanied the possibility of cancer; she is saved from the imaginings of her mind. The angels of her childhood return, an image of her world before the confrontation with the old jacket and the death of God. In expressing her relief Simone de Beauvoir expresses her weakness: the inability to assimilate experiences of anguish to her other experiences. "Wonder" and "whole" take us back to the young child raised in the Catholic bourgeoisie. Nothing suggests that the narrator has grown emotionally beyond this stage. The anguish is always too great to be confronted and absorbed.

There is little anguish involved in the two nearly fatal accidents reported in *La Force de l'âge*. The first one took place in 1937 during a solitary walking trip in the French Alps. Simone de Beauvoir found herself in a situation where she could move neither up nor down. She dropped her knapsack and shortly after tumbled down. " 'Well,' I thought, 'it's happened, and it's happened to me: this is the end!' " [17] When she arrives, scratched but alive, at the bottom of the ravine she is amazed "that I had felt so little emotional reaction when I believed myself on the very brink of death." [18] She trots off for a good night's sleep and starts out on other paths the following morning.

The second accident took place in 1941 during a bicycle trip with Sartre. They were on their way to Grenoble to visit a friend when they met two cyclists coming the other way. Simone de Beauvoir attempted to avoid them, but she did so by moving to the left instead of to the right. In her effort to avoid a head-on collision she braked suddenly, skidded, and then fainted. " 'So this is death,' I thought, and died." [19] Again she is not dead, but badly bruised. Again she continues the trip without fear.

During and after both accidents her reactions were the same. The certitude of death was not accompanied by any fear of it. When the danger was past there was no concern that it would return. Clearly Simone de Beauvoir is not plagued by fears but by anguish. She has little imagination for physical accidents. Her anguish about death has nothing to do with the fact of death or the moment of dying. There is no relation in tone or style between the passages that describe these accidents in which she was near death and the passages in which she is seized by anguish.

The last pages of *La Force de l'âge* reiterate the omnipresent anguish of death, which is, as we have seen so many times, the horror of contemplating her own nonexistence. Simone de Beauvoir understands the difference between the fear and the anguish of death. She sees how her reactions at critical moments differ from her reactions when she attempts to imagine her own nothingness, her absence:

What I rejected, with all my heart and soul, was the horror of that endless night, which, since it did not exist, would never *be* horrible, but held infinite horror for me, who *did* exist. I could not bear to think of myself as finite and ephemeral, a drop of water in the ocean; at times all my endeavors seemed vanity, happiness became a false lure, and the world wore the mocking, illusory mask of Nothingness.[20]

The problem for Simone de Beauvoir is that she can tolerate neither the feeling of insignificance nor the notion of happiness, her happiness, as an illusion. Her fight against nothingness, both in her writings and in her evening tussles with death, cannot be considered a sign of strength but rather a sign of weakness. She is fighting against a vision of what it really means to be mortal.

In her long and impressive documentary essay on old age, *La Vieillesse*, this weakness is blatant.

The evidence I have shows that the fear of death does not generally coincide with an ardent love of life: on the contrary. "The idea of death made my head spin because I didn't love life," writes Sartre about his childhood. Anxious parents, like anxious couples are not those that love the most, but those who find that something is lacking in their feelings. People who are ill at ease with themselves are those who constantly meditate about their death. And we must not think that those who—like Lamartine— call on death with much fanfare really desire death: by speaking about it all the time they only reveal that death obsesses them.[21]

Sartre and unreliable analogies are the final authority. Equivocation replaces serious argument. No one would deny the subjective nature of obsessive anguish, but, the fear of death is not what makes death the essential question. Sartre and Simone de Beauvoir explain their obsession in terms of current ideologies and then put death aside. It does not go away. The value of *La Vieillesse* is diminished because death is both omnipresent and ignored. The inability to move from the fear of one's own physical death and disappearance to the continuous awareness of mortality is a symptom of intellectual paralysis. Simone de Beauvoir never gets beyond the first stage, and consequently her essay with its mass of interesting facts remains on the outskirts of the central problem.

The betrayal of mortality is completed in an earlier essay, "La Pensée de droite aujourd'hui":

"A revolver is solid, it's made of steel, it's an object. At last, the contact with an object," wrote Drieu [La Rochelle] at the end of *Feu follet*. Thus he tells us the fundamental reason for the fascination that death exerts over a right-winger; it's the only *real* event that can take place in a life closed in on its own immanence, a life without content. Cut off from the world, cut off from his fellow men who are all strangers, without love, without a goal, the right-winger is imprisoned in an empty subjectivity where nothing takes place except in his head; only death *happens* to him though it comes from within. He is absolutely alone, without any relation to others, without direction, without a future. Death is responsible for the definite separation. Each man dies alone. That is why the right-winger decides to see in death the truth of life; death confirms his notion that each one lives alone, separate; in its light I depend only on myself. This self is foreign to all those who are foreign to my death; to all. . . . Meditation on death is the supreme wisdom of those who are already dead.[22]

This ideological argument would, of course, place Simone de Beauvoir in the same camp as those she is attacking. The portrait she draws of "the right-winger" is an acceptable portrait of her own metaphysical and psychological orientation. What is the validity of her accusation? Is the preoccupation with death reserved for the right-wing bourgeois? And is it then an inevitable conditioned preoccupation? A form of social alienation? Yes, according to a Marxist interpretation of human behavior. But Marx was understandably so intent on combatting the old theology that he eliminated not only the answers but the questions that prompted them. No, if we study the available anthropological data on human societies. In all of them some provision is made for a flight from death, for a denial of mortality. The one who questions the flight and chooses to encounter mortality would indeed be alienated from the collectivity. He or she would also be in some manner detached from the business of living as it is prescribed by the prevailing structures and values. The term "right-winger" with its strong pejorative charge is quite inappropriate. It can only suggest how violent is Simone de Beauvoir's own preoccupation with death and how gullibly she will employ any argument to aid her in her flight.

The arguments and the flight are doomed. The body of her writings is a "meditation on death"; all her themes and elaborations are pretexts for the endless wrestling with her own mortality, of which she is acutely aware but which she has no means, emotional or intellectual, of confronting without hysteria or ideology.

Awareness is obviously insufficient. Everything in Simone de Beauvoir's childhood contradicts mortality from the egotism nurtured in the child to the instilled notions of heaven and immortal souls. Her evasions are attributes of her conditioning. It is viscerally impossible for her not to erect some line of defense.

The desire to succeed in the eyes of God, or "others," or History through the creation of an image of the self is related both to a certain exigency of the ego that cries out in vanity for an audience and to the dread of death. The very notion of personal success is linked to the notion of personal death. The urge to build an image of the self as a bulwark against eventual nonexistence is finally destructive. The more unique Simone de Beauvoir becomes the more unpalatable death is for her. That is one of the major conclusions of this study.

The importance of Simone de Beauvoir as a writer is paradoxically in this tension between a sense of the absurd and the need for commitment. Simone de Beauvoir's evasions point to the crux of the modern sensibility: the preoccupation with death and the inability to draw all the consequences from the fact and the shadow of mortality.

Simone de Beauvoir

In the same way George Sand, whose life like all lives was mediocre, misshapen, and incomplete, was able to create the unique figure of Consuelo a model in whom every woman finds something to imitate and every man the means to understand and to love every woman.

—Alain, *Propos de littérature*

Her life was a failure, like every life, but on a grand scale.
—Maurois, *Lélia*

Name: Simone de Beauvoir
Date of Birth: January 2, 1908
Place of Birth: Paris, France
Religion: Catholic at birth. None
Marital Status: Single
Profession: Writer, teacher, lecturer
Mother's Name: Françoise de Beauvoir. Deceased
Father's Name: Georges de Beauvoir. Deceased
Siblings: A married sister. Hélène de Beauvoir (de Roulet), painter

Major Works

L'Invitée. Paris, Gallimard, 1943, à Olga Kosakievicz
She Came to Stay. Cleveland and New York, World Publishing Company, 1954

Pyrrhus et Cinéas. Paris, Gallimard, 1944, à cette dame

Le Sang des autres. Paris, Gallimard, 1945, à Nathalie Sorokine
The Blood of Others. Translated by Yvonne Moyse and Roger Senhouse. New York, Alfred A. Knopf, 1948

Les Bouches inutiles. Paris, Gallimard, 1945, à ma mère

Tous les Hommes sont mortels. Paris, Gallimard, 1946, à Jean-Paul Sartre
All Men Are Mortal. Translated by Leonard M. Friedman. Cleveland and New York, World Publishing Company, 1955

Pour une morale de l'ambiguïté. Paris, Gallimard, 1947, à Bianca
The Ethics of Ambiguity. Translated by Bernard Frechtman. New York, Philosophical Library, 1948

L'Amérique au jour le jour. Paris, Gallimard (1948), 1954, à Ellen et Richard Wright
America Day by Day. Translated by Patrick Dudley. New York, Grove Press, 1953

L'Existentialisme et la sagesse des nations, "Idéalisme moral et réalisme politique," "Littérature et métaphysique," "Oeil pour oeil." Paris, Nagel, 1948, à Hélène et Lionel

Le Deuxième Sexe. Paris, Gallimard, 1949, à Jacques Bost
The Second Sex. Translated by H. M. Parshley. New York, Alfred A. Knopf, 1971

Les Mandarins. Paris, Gallimard, 1954, à Nelson Algren
The Mandarins. Translated by Leonard M. Friedman. Cleveland and New York, World Publishing Company, 1956

Privilèges, "Faut-il brûler Sade?" "La Pensée de droite, aujourd'hui," "Merleau-Ponty et le pseudo-sartrisme." Paris, Gallimard, 1955
Must We Burn Sade? Translated by Annette Michelson. London, Peter Nevill Ltd., 1953

La Longue Marche. Paris, Gallimard, 1957
The Long March. Translated by Austryn Wainhouse. Cleveland and New York, World Publishing Company, 1958

Mémoires d'une jeune fille rangée. Paris, Gallimard, 1958
Memoirs of a Dutiful Daughter. Translated by James Kirup. Cleveland and New York, World Publishing Company, 1959

La Force de l'âge. Paris, Gallimard, 1960, à Jean-Paul Sartre
The Prime of Life. Translated by Peter Green. Cleveland and New York, World Publishing Company, 1962

La Force des choses. Paris, Gallimard, 1958
Force of Circumstance. Translated by Richard Howard. New York, G. P. Putnam's Sons, 1964

Une Mort très douce. Paris, Gallimard, 1964, à ma soeur
A Very Easy Death. Translated by Patrick O'Brian. New York, G. P. Putnam's Sons, 1966

Les Belles Images. Paris, Gallimard, 1966, à Claude Lanzmann
Les Belles Images. Translated by Patrick O'Brian. New York, 1968, G. P. Putnam's Sons

La Femme rompue. Paris, Gallimard, 1967
The Woman Destroyed. Translated by Patrick O'Brian. London, Collins, 1968

La Vieillesse. Paris, Gallimard, 1970
The Coming of Age. Translated by Patrick O'Brian. New York, G. P. Putnam's Sons, 1972

I have listed the English-language editions that I have used or consulted. They are not necessarily the first editions.

For a fairly complete bibliography consult *Simone de Beauvoir*, by Serge Julienne-Caffié. La Bibliothèque idéale. Paris, Gallimard, 1966.

Word Portraits

A free independent woman, anarchistic, a bit bohemian, who refuses marriage and maternity, leads an unrestrained life without caring about respectability, money or class, and with a scarf wound like a turban around her head spends her days at cafés writing embarassingly candid novels and arrogant essays in which she preaches atheism, revolt and revolution.

Pierre de Boisdeffre, *Dictionnaire de littérature contemporaine*

The lips are curved into an obliging, fixed half-smile. The grey hair is coiffured with mathematical precision, cleft exactly by the part. At the neck, not entirely masked by the photographer's shadows, a few lines can be discerned. The dress is severe, revealing nothing, so dark that it blends into the background, relieved by a link necklace from which depend castings of the Greek letter epsilon. The whole suggests someone's amiable grandmother, intelligent, well-preserved, still vigorous and minutely intent on keeping up appearances.

Time, May 14, 1965

Simone de Beauvoir's eyes were lit by a light-blue intelligence: she was possessed by something like total apprehension. Her judgments seemed a fraction sooner than immediate and her decisiveness shook the *arrondissement*. . . . Friends sometimes had to remind her that it might be just as well to hang up last winter's dress, midsummer having come to France. Most Parisian of Parisians, she was least the *Parisienne*.

Nelson Algren, *Who Lost an American?*
New York, Macmillan, 1963

Apart from her classically-featured face, what strikes one about Simone de Beauvoir is her fresh, rosy complexion and her clear, blue eyes, extremely young and lively. One gets the impression that she knows and sees everything: this inspires a certain timidity. Her speech is rapid, her manner direct without being brusque, and she is rather smiling and friendly.

"Simone de Beauvoir, an Interview," by Madeleine Gobeil,
translated by Bernard Frechtman.
The Paris Review, No. 34, Spring–Summer, 1965

There is no complete picture, only partial memories. An unknown young woman with a thin open face who came up to us, a long time ago, in a small rundown teacher's lounge where the October sun was dozing. She seemed excessively well-mannered except for her raucous, rapid speech which was not. . . . The face disappears. There are the places where we were together and no longer face to face. From that time on we saw only her eyes, inseparable from her voice and from what her voice said, from the cutting tone of her affirmations, from her naïve concentration when she was asked a question, from her slightly aggressive timidity when she confided in you. Someone with whom we would never tire of speaking and who stimulated in us a strong critical sense in relation to ourselves and to the world. In short, one of the rare persons who justified our sojourn on this earth.

Colette Audry. "Portrait de l'écrivain jeune femme,"
Livres de France, Novembre, 1962

Gobeil: What do you think of Simone de Beauvoir as a woman?
Sartre: I think she's beautiful. I've always thought her beautiful, even though she was wearing a hideous little hat when I first met her. I was dead set on making her acquaintance because she was beautiful, because she had, and still has, the kind of face that appeals to me. The wonderful thing about Simone de Beauvoir is that she has a man's intelligence—you can see from the way I'm talking that I'm still a bit feudal—and a woman's sensitivity. That is I've found in her everything I could possibly want.

"Sartre talks of Beauvoir," An Interview with Madeleine Gobeil,
translated by Bernard Frechtman. *Vogue*, July, 1964

Jean-Paul Sartre and Simone de Beauvoir are God's orphans; perhaps because they refuse the simple love that creates men.

Having rejected their family tradition, having no child's face near them, having no future other than in their books they are really alone and consequently, or so it seems to me, they are naturally insensitive to God.

Georges Hourdin, *Simone de Beauvoir et la liberté*.
Paris, Les Editions du Cerf, 1962

When we have finished reading the works of this woman writer we carry away with us the varied odors of the earth, the taste of life and of death, the echoes of a voice that will never leave us and which repeats to us every day that *the force of circumstance* is in fact inextricably tied to *the weakness of man*.

Laurent Gagnebin, *Simone de Beauvoir*.
Paris, Editions Fischbacher, 1962

If I add that she has explored the entire planet, that she has had the occasion to meet most of the people who comprise, in all domains, the true elite of this world, that her political, philosophical, literary, artistic and cinematographic culture is unbelievable and that her passion for what is going on (minor or major events) has not diminished, how will I succeed in justifying to the reader the undertaking that I am asking him to judge?

Francis Jeanson, *Simone de Beauvoir ou l'entreprise de vivre*.
Paris, Editions du Seuil, 1966

Résumé

A résumé of the essential facts and circumstances of Simone de Beauvoir's life based on the first three volumes of her memoirs:

A young, highly intelligent girl, raised in the Catholic faith and in an ultranationalistic milieu, dimly aware at an early age of the discrepancy between the pagan ethics of her father and the rigid moral conventionalism of her mother, she began by rejecting the God of her mother, then the chauvinism and brittle charm of her father and finally all the values that she associated with the bourgeoisie. She spent her winters in Paris, at first protected by a nursemaid Louise and her parents and grandparents within the confines of an apartment on the Boulevard Raspail, later protected by the school-teachers of the Catholic Cours Désir. She spent her summers in the provinces, usually at her paternal uncle's estate in the Limousin, where she played with her cousin and her sister, or read, or became involved with the sights and smells of the countryside. She began to write when she was eight years old. At the age of fifteen she discovered that she was, like all human beings, condemned to death. She had a childhood friend Zaza, whom she dearly loved; she had an older cousin Jacques, whom she adored and contemplated marrying; she had a professor of literature, Robert Garric, "a man who instead of submitting to fate had chosen his way of life," whom she worshipped. In the hope of attracting Garric's attention she joined his Social Service Group and had her initiation among the poor. The friend died; the cousin had a mistress; Garric was inaccessible and a fervent Catholic. At the Sorbonne, where she studied Greek and philology and specialized in philosophy, she met students from different backgrounds and with different mores. She formed with one of them, the most outstanding and least conventional, Jean-Paul Sartre, a lasting alliance. She worked diligently, read omnivorously, passed all her examinations brilliantly. At the threshold of adulthood she was equipped to be a professor of philosophy in the French lycée system.

She taught initially at Marseille, where she explored the surrounding countryside on foot with insistent regularity. After a year at Marseille she was named to a post at Rouen, thus much closer to Sartre, who was at Le Havre. At Rouen she continued to write, to read, and to walk during her vacations in France and in Europe. She also became embroiled in the lives of her colleagues and students. During those years at Rouen (1933–37) a war was being prepared for all Europe and tried out in Spain. Sartre and Simone de Beauvoir were both impervious to the march of history and sympathetic to all revolutionary movements. Sartre suffered from severe depression and was pursued for almost a year by visions of lobsters; at the same time he formed with Simone de Beauvoir and one of her students an experimental and ill-fated trio. Paris followed Rouen. Simone de Beauvoir continued to teach philosophy, occasionally with great enthusiasm, to write, walk, read, listen to records, frequent the cinemas, theaters, art galleries, and cafés, to travel, ski, and to talk interminably with old and new students and always with Sartre. The war came and the painful defeat of France and with them the realization that History was an active, vital force that determined the shape of their destinies whether or not they acknowledged it. During the period of the German occupation of France, Simone de Beauvoir completed her first novel, and her literary fame, together with Sartre's greater fame and their marginal activities in the Resistance movement, brought them into contact with new people and prominent figures. The second volume of the memoirs ends with the liberation of Paris, the exaltation of Simone de Beauvoir, and a long meditation on death.

The third and last volume is divided into two parts and takes us from the liberation of Paris in 1944 to the end of the Algerian war in 1962. The first part, from 1944 to 1952, begins on a note of hopeful exuberance. For both political and personal reasons this exuberance is short-lived. The unity created by the Resistance movement dissolved with the defeat of the enemy; the end of the occupation was also the end of an ideal. In 1945, Sartre, during his first voyage to America, began a liaison of considerable importance to him and of considerable concern to Simone de Beauvoir. In 1947 Simone de Beauvoir, during her first voyage to America, likewise began a liaison which, despite crises and tears, provided sufficient excitement abroad to counteract, for a time, the disenchantment at home.

In the second part of the third volume, *Force of Circumstance*, the events are overwhelming. Of these the most painful for Simone de Beauvoir are Sartre's often precarious health, the protracted Algerian war, and her psychological adaptation to the physiology of old age. These circumstances do not, however, prevent her from writing, from participating in the antiwar movement, from falling in love with a man twenty-five years her junior, from travelling in the United States, China, the Soviet Union, Scandinavia, Cuba, Brazil and every summer with Sartre to her favorite city Rome. As Simone de Beauvoir comes into closer contact with certain truths, the hunger of two-thirds of the earth's inhabitants, her own and Sartre's imminent death, she becomes increasingly poignant and dogmatic. At the end of the third volume the aging, sensitive, lucid woman and the truculent neo-Marxist alternate in cries of hope and despair for the human situation, which can be improved, and the human condition, which cannot be.

Notes

1. "Comment tirerait-on de soi de bonnes raisons de vivre?" dit-elle, "puisqu'on meurt."
   "Ça ne change rien."
   "Moi, je trouve que ça change tout," dit-elle. Elle me dévisagea avec curiosité. "Ça vous est égal de penser qu'un jour vous ne serez plus là, qu'il n'y aura même plus personne pour penser à vous?"
   "Si j'ai vécu comme je voulais, qu'importe?"
   "Mais une vie, pour que ce soit intéressant, il faudrait que ça ressemble à une ascension: on franchit un palier puis un autre, puis un autre et chacun n'est fait que pour le palier suivant." Elle haussa les épaules. "Alors, si une fois au sommet tout s'effondre—ça devient absurde depuis le début. Vous ne trouvez pas?"
   "Non," dis-je distraitement!
   Le Sang des autres, pp. 67–68
   The Blood of Others, p. 84

2. "Sauvez-moi," dit-elle. "Sauvez-moi de la mort."
   Tous les Hommes sont mortels, p. 42

3. . . . je pensai, quand je me couchai pour la première fois dans ma nouvelle chambre, "Voilà mon lit de mort."
   La Force des choses, pp. 366–367
   Force of Circumstance, p. 343

4. J'ai passé les vingt premières années de ma vie dans un gros village qui s'étendait du Lion de Belfort à la rue Jacob, du boulevard Saint-Germain au boulevard Raspail: j'y habite encore.

La Force des choses, p. 393
Force of Circumstance, p. 371

5. Une nuit, en juin 1944, j'ai tenté de conjurer la mort avec des mots. Je détache quelques-unes de ces notes, telles que je les pris au courant de la plume . . .

La Force de l'âge, p. 617
The Prime of Life, p. 475

CHAPTER II

1. La maison était vide; on avait fermé les volets à cause du soleil et il faisait sombre; sur le palier du premier étage, Françoise, collée contre le mur, retenait sa respiration. Tout à l'heure il y avait eu le craquement des marches de l'escalier et puis le craquement des vieilles lattes du plancher et les vitres de la bibliothèque avaient un peu tremblé; maintenant on n'entendait plus rien du tout. La porte de ma chambre, la porte des cabinets, la chambre de grand-mère, la chambre de papa et maman. C'était drôle de se trouver là toute seule alors que tout le monde était dans le jardin; c'était drôle et ça faisait peur. Les meubles avaient leur air de tous les jours, mais en même temps ils étaient tout changés; tout épais, tout lourds, tout secrets; sous la bibliothèque et sous la console de marbre stagnait une ombre épaisse. On n'avait pas envie de se sauver, mais on se sentait le cœur serré.

Le vieux veston était suspendu au dossier d'une chaise; sans doute Anna l'avait nettoyé à l'essence, ou encore elle venait de le sortir de la naphtaline et elle l'avait mis là à prendre l'air; il était très vieux, il avait l'air fatigué. Il était vieux et fatigué mais il ne pouvait pas se plaindre comme Françoise se plaignait quand elle s'était fait mal: il n'avait pas d'âme; il ne pouvait pas se dire "je suis un vieux veston fatigué." C'était étrange; Françoise essaya d'imaginer comment ça lui ferait si elle ne pouvait pas dire "je suis Françoise, j'ai six ans, je suis dans la maison de grand-mère"; si elle ne pouvait absolument rien se dire; elle ferma les yeux. C'est comme si on n'existait pas; et pourtant d'autres gens viendraient là, ils me verraient et ils parleraient de moi. Elle ouvrit les yeux; elle voyait le veston, il existait et il ne s'en rendait pas compte, il y avait là quelque chose d'irritant, d'un peu effrayant.

A quoi ça lui sert d'exister, s'il ne sait pas? Elle réfléchit: peut-
être il y aurait un moyen. "Puisque moi, je peux dire 'moi'; si je le
disais pour lui?" C'était plutôt désappointant; elle avait beau regarder le veston, ne plus voir que lui et dire très vite, "je suis
vieux, je suis fatigué"; il ne se passait rien de neuf; le veston
restait là, indifférent, tout étranger, et elle était toujours Françoise.
D'ailleurs, si elle devenait un moment le veston, alors elle, Françoise, elle n'en saurait plus rien. Tout se mit à tourner dans sa tête
comme quand elle avait fait une grosse colère et qu'elle se
retrouvait, à bout de larmes et de cris, couché sur le plancher.
Elle entra dans la chambre de sa mère, prit le livre qu'elle était
venue chercher et redescendit en courant au jardin.

"L'Enfance de Françoise Miquel"
(Unpublished)

2. Une angoisse la traversa: ce n'était pas une souffrance
précise, il fallait remonter très loin pour retrouver un pareil
malaise. Un souvenir lui revint. La maison était vide; on avait
fermé les volets à cause du soleil et il faisait sombre; sur le palier
du premier étage, une petite fille collée contre le mur retenait sa
respiration. C'était drôle de se trouver là toute seule alors que tout
le monde était dans le jardin, c'était drôle et ça faisait peur; les
meubles avaient leur air de tous les jours, mais en même temps
ils étaient tout changés: tout épais, tout lourds, tout secrets; sous
la bibliothèque et sous la console de marbre stagnait une ombre
épaisse. On n'avait pas envie de se sauver mais on se sentait le
coeur serré.

Le vieux veston était suspendu au dossier d'une chaise: sans
doute Anna l'avait nettoyé à l'essence, ou encore elle venait de le
sortir de la naphtaline et elle l'avait mis là à prendre l'air; il était
très vieux, il avait l'air très fatigué. Il était vieux et fatigué mais
il ne pouvait pas se plaindre comme Françoise se plaignait quand
elle s'était fait mal, il ne pouvait pas se dire "je suis un vieux veston fatigué." C'était étrange; Françoise essaya d'imaginer comment ça lui ferait si elle ne pouvait pas se dire "je suis Françoise,
j'ai six ans, je suis dans la maison de grand-mère," si elle ne
pouvait absolument rien se dire; elle ferma les yeux. C'est comme
si on n'existait pas; et pourtant d'autres gens viendraient là, ils me
verraient, ils parleraient de moi. Elle ouvrit les yeux; elle voyait
le veston, il existait et il ne s'en rendait pas compte, il y avait la
quelque chose d'irritant, d'un peu effrayant. A quoi ça lui sert
d'exister s'il ne sait pas? Elle réfléchit; peut-être il y aurait un

moyen. Puisque moi je peux dire "moi," si je le disais pour lui? C'était plutôt désappointant; elle avait beau regarder le veston, ne plus voir que lui et dire très vite: "Je suis vieux, je suis fatigué," il ne se passait rien de neuf; le veston restait là, indifférent, tout étranger, et elle était toujours Françoise. D'ailleurs, si elle devenait le veston, alors elle, Françoise, n'en saurait plus rien. Tout se mit à tourner dans sa tête et elle redescendit en courant au jardin.

L'Invitée, pp. 128–129
She Came to Stay, p. 120

3. J'ai raconté ailleurs comment, à Meyrignac, je contemplai stupidement un vieux veston abandonné sur le dossier d'une chaise. J'essayai de dire à sa place: "Je suis un vieux veston fatigué." C'était impossible et la panique me prit. Dans les siècles révolus, dans le silence des êtres inanimés je pressentais ma propre absence: je pressentais la vérité, fallacieusement conjurée, de ma mort."

Mémoires d'une jeune fille rangée, p. 51
Memoirs of a Dutiful Daughter, p. 53

4. En particulier, il arrive souvent aux enfants qui ne sont pas encore ancrés dans leur petit coin d'univers d'éprouver avec étonnement leur "être dans le monde" comme ils éprouvent leur corps. Par exemple, c'est une expérience métaphysique que cette découverte de "l'ipséité" décrite par Lewis Carroll dans *Alice au pays des Merveilles*, par Richard Hughes dans *Un Cyclone à la Jamaïque;* l'enfant découvre concrètement sa présence au monde, son délaissement, sa liberté, l'opacité des choses, la résistance des consciences étrangères.

"Littérature et métaphysique," in *L'Existentialisme et la sagesse des nations*, p. 115

Chapter III

1. Ç'a été ma première déception touchant la religion et les prêtres et je ne m'en suis jamais bien relevée. J'avais si longtemps dans ma pensée confondu Dieu et l'Abbé Mirande que j'ai commencé à me demander si Dieu n'était pas lui aussi du côté de maman, des vieilles maniaques qui tenaient l'Institut Joliet, des livres marqués J sur le catalogue de la bibliothèque des Familles; mais ce Dieu était si absurde que j'ai bientôt douté qu'il existât. La première fois que ce doute m'a envahi, j'ai eu bien peur; c'était à la campagne, j'étais couchée sur la mousse, la cime d'un bouleau

se balançait au-dessus de ma tête; je n'ai rien pensé, mais au milieu d'un grand silence il m'a semblé que le monde venait soudain de se vider; les arbres, le ciel, l'herbe, personne ne leur ordonner d'exister, et moi-même je flottais par hasard parmi ces vagues aspects du néant; je me suis levée, je ne pouvais pas supporter cette angoisse; j'ai couru vers la maison, vers des voix humaines. Ça fait drôle, après avoir vécu dans un monde peuplé d'anges et de saints sous le regard d'un être tout puissant de se trouver soudain seule parmi des choses aveugles.

"Marguerite," in "La Primauté du spirituel," pp. 223–224

2. Non, ce n'est pas aujourd'hui que je connaîtrai ma mort; ni aujourd'hui ni aucun jour. Je serai morte pour les autres sans jamais m'être vue mourir.

J'ai refermé les yeux, mais sans pouvoir me rendormir. Pourquoi la mort a-t-elle de nouveau traversé mes rêves? Elle rôde, je la sens qui rôde. Pourquoi?

Je n'ai pas toujours su que je mourrais. Enfant, j'ai cru en Dieu. Une robe blanche et deux ailes lustrées m'attendaient dans les vestiaires du ciel: je souhaitais crever les nuées. Je m'étendais sur mon édredon, les mains jointes, et je m'abandonnais aux délices de l'au-delà. Parfois dans mon sommeil je me disais: "Je suis morte" et ma voix vigilante me garantissait l'éternité. Le silence de la mort, c'est avec horreur que je l'ai découvert. Une sirène expirait au bord de la mer; pour l'amour d'un jeune homme elle avait renoncé à son âme immortelle et il ne restait d'elle qu'un peu d'écume blanche sans souvenir, sans voix. Je me disais pour me rassurer: "C'est un conte!"

Ce n'était pas un conte. C'est moi la sirène, Dieu est devenu une idée abstraite au fond du ciel et un soir je l'ai effacée. Je n'ai jamais regretté Dieu: il me volait la terre. Mais un jour j'ai compris qu'en renonçant à lui je m'étais condamnée à mort; j'avais quinze ans; dans l'appartement désert, j'ai crié. En reprenant mes sens, je me suis demandé: "Comment les autres gens font-ils? Comment ferai-je? Est-ce que je vais vivre avec cette peur?"

Du moment où j'ai aimé Robert, je n'ai plus jamais eu peur, de rien.

Les Mandarins, pp. 26–27
The Mandarins, pp. 30–31

3. J'envisageais la vie comme une aventure heureuse; contre la mort, la foi me défendait: je fermerais les yeux, et en un éclair,

les mains neigeuses des anges me transporteraient au ciel. . . .
souvent je me couchais sur la moquette, yeux clos, mains jointes,
et je commandais à mon âme de s'échapper. Ce n'était qu'un jeu:
si j'avais cru ma dernière heure venue, j'aurais crié de terreur.
Du moins l'idée de la mort ne m'effrayait–elle pas. Un soir pourtant, le néant m'a transie. Je lisais: au bord de la mer, une sirène
expirait; pour l'amour d'un beau prince, elle avait renoncé à son
âme immortelle, elle se changeait en écume. Cette voix qui en elle
répétait sans trêve: "Je suis là," s'était tue pour toujours: il me
sembla que l'univers entier avait sombré dans le silence. Mais non.
Dieu me promettait l'éternité: jamais je ne cesserais de voir,
d'entendre, de me parler. Il n'y aurait pas de fin. . . .

Je me perdais jusqu'au vertige dans ces rêveries oiseuses, niant
vainement le scandaleux divorce de ma conscience et du temps.

Mémoires d'une jeune fille rangée, pp. 50–51
Memoirs of a Dutiful Daughter, pp. 51–53

4. Cependant la face de l'univers changea. Plus d'une fois, dans
les jours qui suivirent, assise au pied du hêtre pourpre ou des
peupliers argentés, je ressentis dans l'angoisse le vide du ciel.
Naguère, je me tenais au centre d'un vivant tableau dont Dieu
même avait choisi les couleurs et les lumières; toutes les choses
fredonnaient doucement sa gloire. Soudain, tout se taisait. Quel
silence! La terre roulait dans un espace que nul regard ne trans-
perçait, et perdue sur sa surface immense, au milieu de l'éther
aveugle, j'étais seule. Seule: pour la première fois je comprenais
le sens terrible de ce mot. Seule: sans témoin, sans interlocuteur,
sans recours. Mon souffle dans ma poitrine, mon sang dans mes
veines, et ce remue-ménage dans ma tête, cela n'existait pour
personne. Je me levais, je courais vers le parc, je m'asseyais sous
le catalpa entre maman et tante Marguerite tant j'avais besoin
d'entendre des voix.

Je fis une autre découverte. Un après-midi, à Paris, je réalisai
que j'étais condamnée à mort. Il n'y avait personne que moi dans
l'appartement et je ne refrénai pas mon désespoir; j'ai crié, j'ai
griffé la moquette rouge. Et quand je me relevai, hébétée, je me
demandai: "Comment les autres gens font-ils? Comment ferai-je?"
Il me semblait impossible de vivre toute ma vie le coeur tordu
par l'horreur. Quand l'échéance s'approche, me disais-je, quand
on a déjà trente ans, quarante ans et qu'on pense: "C'est pour
demain," comment le supporte-t-on? Plus que la mort elle-même

je redoutais cette épouvante qui bientôt serait mon lot, et pour toujours.

Heureusement, au cours de l'année scolaire, ces fulgurations métaphysiques se firent rares: je manquais de loisir et de solitude. Quant à la pratique de ma vie, ma conversion ne la modifia pas. J'avais cessé de croire en découvrant que Dieu n'exerçait aucune influence sur mes conduites: elles ne changèrent donc pas lorsque je renonçai à lui. J'avais imaginé que la loi morale tenait de lui sa nécessité: mais elle s'était si profondément gravée en moi qu'elle demeura intacte après sa suppression.

> *Mémoires d'une jeune fille rangée*, p. 139
> *Memoirs of a Dutiful Daughter*, pp. 145–146

5. "... Pour moi, son existence [celle de Sartre] justifiait le monde que rien ne justifiait à ses yeux."

> *La Force de l'âge*, p. 220

Chapter IV

1. J'ai connu un enfant qui pleurait parce que le fils de sa concierge était mort; ses parents l'ont laissé pleurer, et puis ils se sont agacés, "Après tout ce petit garçon n'était pas ton frère." L'enfant a essuyé ses larmes. Mais c'était là un enseignement dangereux. Inutile de pleurer sur un petit garçon étranger: Soit. Mais pourquoi pleurer sur son frère?

> *Pyrrhus et Cinéas*, p. 13

2. J'avais huit ans quand pour la première fois mon coeur a connu le scandale. J'étais en train de lire dans la galerie; ma mère est rentrée avec un de ces visages que nous lui voyions souvent, un visage chargé de reproche et d'excuse et elle a dit: "Le petit de Louise est mort." Je revois l'escalier tordu et le corridor dallé sur lequel donnaient tant de portes, toutes pareilles; maman m'a dit que derrière chaque porte il y avait une chambre où toute une famille habitait. Nous sommes entrés. Louise m'a pris dans ses bras; ses joues étaient molles et mouillées; maman s'est assise sur le lit, à côté d'elle, et s'est mise a lui parler à voix basse. Dans le moïse, il y avait un bébé pâle aux yeux fermés. J'ai regardé le carreau rouge, les murs nus, le réchaud à gaz et je me suis mis à pleurer. Je pleurais et maman parlait, et l'enfant restait mort. Je pouvais bien vider ma tirelire, et maman pouvait veiller des nuits entières: il serait toujours aussi mort.

"Qu'est-ce qu'il a cet enfant?" dit mon père.

"Il m'a accompagné chez Louise," dit maman.

Elle avait déjà raconté l'histoire, mais de nouveau elle essayait de la faire sentir, avec des mots: la méningite, la nuit angoissée, et au matin le petit corps raidi. Papa écoutait en mangeant son potage. Je ne pouvais pas manger. Là-bas, Louise pleurait, elle ne mangeait pas; rien ne lui rendrait son enfant, jamais; rien n'effacerait ce malheur qui souillait le monde.

"Eh bien! mange ta soupe," dit mon père. "Tout le monde a fini."

"Je n'ai pas faim."

"Force-toi un peu, mon chéri," dit maman.

Je portai la cuiller à mes lèvres et la reposai sur l'assiette avec une espèce de hoquet:

"Je ne peux pas!"

"Ecoute," dit mon père. "C'est très triste que le petit de Louise soit mort, j'en suis navré pour elle, mais nous n'allons pas le pleurer toute notre vie. Allons, dépêche-toi un peu." J'ai mangé. D'un seul coup, la voix dure a desserré cet étau autour de ma gorge. Je sentais le liquide tiède glisser contre les muqueuses et avec chaque cuillerée coulait en moi quelque chose de plus nauséabond que l'odeur de l'imprimerie. Mais l'étau s'était desserré. Pas toute notre vie. *Cette nuit jusqu'à l'aube et quelques jours peut-être. Mais pas toute la vie. Après tout, c'est son malheur et non le nôtre. C'est sa mort. Ils l'avaient couché sur le banc avec son col déchiré et ce sang caillé sur son visage; son sang, pas le mien. "Je n'oublierai jamais." Marcel aussi l'a crié dans son coeur. "Jamais petite tête, petit cheval, bon petit sujet si sage. Jamais ton rire, tes yeux vivants." Et sa mort est au fond de nos vies, paisible et étrangère, et nous, vivants, nous nous la rappelons; nous vivons de nous la rappeler alors qu'elle n'existe plus, qu'elle n'a jamais existé pour lui qui est mort. Pas toute notre vie. Pas même quelques jours. Pas même une minute. Tu es seule sur ce lit, et moi je ne peux qu'entendre ce râle qui sort de tes lèvres et que tu n'entends pas.*

Il avait mangé son potage et tout son dîner. Maintenant il était blotti sous le piano à queue: le lustre de cristal brillait de tous ses feux, sous leur carapace de sucre les fruits glacés scintillaient; tendres et coloriées comme les petits fours, les belles dames souriaient. Il regardait sa mère: elle ne ressemblait pas à ces fées parfumées; une robe noire découvrait ses épaules; ses cheveux noirs

comme sa robe s'enroulaient en bandeau moiré autour de sa tête;
mais devant elle, on ne pensait ni à des fleurs, ni à des gâteaux
opulents ni à des coquillages ou à des galets bleutés. Une présence, une pure présence humaine. Elle courait d'un bout à l'autre
du salon, dans ses minuscules souliers de satin aux talons trop
hauts; et elle aussi souriait. Même elle. Tout à l'heure, ce visage
chaviré, cette voix basse et intense qui chuchotait à l'oreille de
Louise; et maintenant ce rire. Pas toute notre vie. Il avait griffé
le tapis. Le petit de Louise est mort. Il se forçait à contempler
l'image: Louise assise au bord du lit qui pleurait. Lui ne pleurait
plus. Et même, à travers l'image figée et transparente, il suivait
des yeux à présent les robes mauves, vertes, roses; et les désirs
renaissaient; désir de mordre dans ces bras crémeux, de plonger
le visage dans ces chevelures, de froisser comme un pétale les
soies légères. Le petit de Louise est mort. En vain. Ce n'est pas
mon malheur. *Ce n'est pas ma mort. Je ferme les yeux, je reste
immobile, mais c'est de moi que je me souviens et sa mort entre
dans ma vie: moi je n'entre pas dans sa mort.* Je me suis faufilé
sous le piano, et dans mon lit j'ai pleuré jusqu'au sommeil à cause
de cette chose qui avait coulé dans ma gorge avec le potage tiède,
plus âcre que le remords: ma faute. La faute de sourire pendant
que Louise pleurait, la faute de pleurer mes larmes et non les
siennes. La faute d'être un autre.

Le Sang des autres, pp. 10–12
The Blood of Others, pp. 7–10

3. Il m'arriva une seule fois de pressentir le dénuement. Louise
habitait avec son mari, le couvreur, une chambre, rue Madame,
sous les toits; elle eut un bébé et j'allai la voir avec ma mère. Je
n'avais jamais mis les pieds dans un sixième. Le triste boyau sur
lequel donnaient une douzaine de portes, toutes semblables, me
serra le coeur. La chambre de Louise, minuscule, contenait un
lit de fer, un berceau, une table qui supportait un réchaud; elle
dormait, cuisinait, mangeait, vivait avec un homme entre ces qua-
tres murs; tout au long du corridor, des familles étouffaient,
claquemurées dans d'identiques réduits; déjà la promiscuité dans
laquelle je vivais et la monotonie des journées bourgeoises m'op-
pressaient. J'entrevis un univers où l'air qu'on respirait avait un
goût de suie, dont nulle lumière jamais ne perçait la crasse: l'existence y était une lente agonie.

A peu de temps de là, Louise perdit son enfant. Je sanglotais pendant des heures: c'était la première fois que je voyais face à face le malheur. J'imaginais Louise dans sa chambre sans joie, privée de son enfant, privée de tout: une telle détresse aurait dû faire exploser la terre. "C'est trop injuste!" me disais-je. Je ne pensais pas seulement à l'enfant mort, mais au corridor du sixième. Je finis par sécher mes larmes sans avoir mis en question la société.

Mémoires d'une jeune fille rangée, pp. 132–133
Memoirs of a Dutiful Daughter, pp. 138–139

4. Mon oncle Maurice après s'être nourri exclusivement de salade pendant deux ou trois ans, était mort d'un cancer à l'estomac, dans des souffrances affreuses. Ma tante et Madeleine l'avait longuement pleuré. Mais quand elles furent consolées, la vie devint, à la Grillère, beaucoup plus gaie que par le passé.

Mémoires d'une jeune fille rangée, p. 164
Memoirs of a Dutiful Daughter, p. 173

5. Bon-papa mourut à la fin de l'automne après une interminable agonie; ma mère s'enveloppa de crêpe et fit teindre en noir mes vêtements. Cette livrée funèbre m'enlaidissait, m'isolait et il me sembla qu'elle me vouait définitivement à une austérité qui commençait à me peser.

Mémoires d'une jeune fille rangée, p. 174
Memoirs of a Dutiful Daughter, p. 184

6. Quelques jours plus tard, je vis pour la première fois de ma vie mourir quelqu'un: mon oncle Gaston, brusquement emporté par une occlusion intestinale. Il agonisa toute une nuit. Tante Marguerite lui tenait la main, et lui disait des mots qu'il n'entendait pas. Ses enfants étaient à son chevet, et mes parents, ma soeur et moi. Il râlait, et il vomissait des choses noires. Quand il s'arrêta de respirer, sa mâchoire pendait, et on noua une mentonnière autour de sa tête. Mon père que je n'avais jamais vu pleurer, sanglotait. La violence de mon désespoir surprit tout le monde et moi-même. J'aimais bien mon oncle, et le souvenir de nos parties de chasse à Meyrignac, dans le petit matin; j'aimais bien ma cousine Jeanne et j'avais horreur de me dire: elle est orpheline. Mais ni mes regrets, ni ma compassion ne justifient l'ouragan qui me dévasta pendant deux jours: je ne supportais pas ce regard noyé que mon oncle avait jeté à sa femme, juste avant de mourir, et où déjà l'irréparable était accompli. Irréparable, irrémédiable: ces mots martelaient ma tête, à la faire éclater; et un autre leur

répondait: inévitable. Peut-être moi aussi je verrais ce regard dans les yeux de l'homme que j'aurais longuement aimé.

Ce fut Jacques qui me consola.

Mémoires d'une jeune fille rangée, p. 214
Memoirs of a Dutiful Daughter, p. 228

7. Le lendemain matin une lettre de Meyrignac m'apprit que grand-père était gravement malade, qu'il allait mourir; je l'aimais bien, mais il était très âgé, sa mort me semblait naturelle et je ne m'en attristais pas. . . . Une dépêche, le dimanche, m'annonça la mort de grand-père; décidément, mon passé se défaisait. . . . A Meyrignac, toute la famille était rassemblée; ce fut peut-être à cause de ce brouhaha que ni la dépouille de grand-père, ni la maison, ni le parc ne m'émurent. . . . J'étais prête à présent pour quelque chose d'autre; dans la violence de cette attente, les regrets s'anéantissaient.

Mémoires d'une jeune fille rangée, pp. 317–319
Memoirs of a Dutiful Daughter, pp. 339–340

CHAPTER V

1. La mort d'Anne fut une surprise: avant d'être transporté à Uzerche son corps fut exposé dans une chapelle ardente. Son visage était jaune et squelettique; les longs cheveux noirs enracinés dans cette chair morte s'étalaient sur l'oreiller cassants, ternes, encore vivants. Pascal pressa ses doigts contre ses paupières; il ne voulait plus regarder ce maigre cadavre qu'entouraient des cierges et des fleurs d'automne; il ne restait rien d'Anne dans cette dépouille charnelle; pour atteindre Anne dans sa vérité essentielle, c'est en son propre coeur qu'il devait la chercher.

"Anne," in "La Primauté du spirituel," p. 208

2. . . . La mort d'Anne lui [Chantal] avait dévoilé la laideur du monde, sa ferveur s'était tarie, elle ne voulait opposer à l'absurdité du destin qu'une amertume lucide.

Ibid., p. 213

3. "C'est la seule consolation qui nous reste," dit Madame Vignon, "de penser que sa mort n'aura pas été inutile à la gloire de Dieu."

Ibid., p. 215

4. . . . Comme Anne était présente, entre ces vieux murs! Ses yeux dorés, ses lourds cheveux bleutés, son visage couleur d'au-

tomne—comme je voudrais pouvoir la faire revivre; il faudrait tout un livre pour la montrer telle que vraiment elle était, un être de chair et de flamme; la belle héroïne claire et mystérieuse avec son rire ingénu, son coeur passionné. Pourquoi s'obstiner à regretter la femme qu'elle serait devenue? Il y avait une mission à remplir envers la pathétique jeune fille dont l'image hantait ce vieux salon . . . dans l'ombre sereine de cette vieille maison elle avait enfin rencontré ce qu'elle cherchait depuis si longtemps; quelque chose qui n'appartînt qu'à elle seule et qu'on pût lui envier; une belle et tragique histoire alourdirait à jamais sa vie; désormais des ombres mystérieuses passeraient parfois sur son visage, ses gestes ses paroles auraient de subtiles résonances et les regards qui se poseraient sur elle s'attarderaient longtemps, avides de percer son secret. La tête de Chantal se courba davantage; il pesait lourd contre son coeur, ce merveilleux fardeau; elle ne pouvait pas prévoir encore toutes les richesses qu'il lui dispenserait, mais elle se sentait déjà transfigurée par sa présence; mieux qu'autrefois elle saurait aimer, comprendre, éclairer, consoler; peut-être même serait-elle capable un jour de transformer sa douleureuse expérience en une oeuvre de sereine beauté.

"Anne chérie, je ne vous oublierai jamais," promit-elle avec ferveur.

Ibid., pp. 215–216

5. Pendant quatre jours, dans la clinique de Saint-Cloud, elle réclama "mon violon, Pradelle, Simone et du champagne." La fièvre ne tomba pas. Sa mère eut le droit de passer la dernière nuit auprès d'elle. Zaza la reconnut et sut qu'elle mourrait. "N'ayez pas de chagrin, maman chérie," dit-elle. "Dans toutes les familles il y a du déchet: c'est moi le déchet."

Quand je la revis, dans la chapelle de la clinique, elle était couchée au milieu d'un parterre de cierges et de fleurs. Elle portait une longue chemise de nuit en toile rêche. Ses cheveux avaient poussé, ils tombaient en mèches raides autour d'un visage jaune, et si maigre, que j'y retrouvai à peine ses traits. Les mains aux longues griffes pâles, croisées sur le crucifix, semblaient friables comme celles d'une très vieille momie. Madame Mabille sanglotait. "Nous n'avons été que les instruments entre les mains de Dieu," lui dit M. Mabille.

Les médecins parlèrent de méningite, d'encéphalite, on ne sut rien de précis. S'agissait-il d'une maladie contagieuse, d'un accident? Ou Zaza avait-elle succombé à un excès de fatigue et d'angoisse? Souvent la nuit elle m'est apparue, toute jaune sous une capeline rose, et elle me regardait avec reproche. Ensemble nous avons lutté contre le destin fangeux qui nous guettait et j'ai pensé longuement que j'avais payé ma liberté de sa mort.

Mémoires d'une jeune fille rangée, pp. 358–359
Memoirs of a Dutiful Daughter, pp. 381–382

6. Roy, Claude, "Beauvoir, par Simone," *La Nef*, No. 22, 1958, pp. 75–78.

7. Je ne m'avisai pas tout de suite de la place que cette amitié tenait dans ma vie; je n'étais guère plus habile que dans ma première enfance à nommer ce qui se passait en moi. On m'avait entraînée à confondre ce qui doit être et ce qui est: je n'examinais pas ce qui se cachait sous la convention des mots. Il était entendu que j'avais une tendre affection pour toute ma famille, y compris mes plus lointains cousins. Mes parents, ma soeur, je les aimais: ce mot couvrait tout. Les nuances de mes sentiments, leurs fluctuations, n'avaient pas droit à l'existence. Zaza était ma meilleure amie: il n'y avait rien de plus à dire. Dans un coeur bien ordonné, l'amitié occupe un rang honorable, mais elle n'a ni l'éclat du mystérieux Amour, ni la dignité sacrée des tendresses filiales. Je ne mettais pas en question cette hiérarchie.

Cette année-là, comme les autres années, le mois d'octobre m'apporta la joyeuse fièvre des rentrées. Les livres neufs craquaient entre les doigts, ils sentaient bon; assise dans le fauteuil de cuir, je me grisai des promesses de l'avenir.

Aucune promesse ne fut tenue. Je retrouvai dans les jardins du Luxembourg l'odeur et les rousseurs de l'automne: elles ne me touchaient plus; le bleu du ciel s'était terni. Les classes m'ennuyèrent; j'apprenais mes leçons, je faisais mes devoirs sans joie, et je poussais avec indifférence la porte du cours Désir. C'était bien mon passé qui ressuscitait et pourtant je ne le reconnaissais pas: il avait perdu toutes ses couleurs; mes journées n'avaient plus de goût. Tout m'était donné, et mes mains restaient vides. Je marchais sur le boulevard Raspail à côté de maman et je me demandai soudain avec angoisse: "Qu'arrive-t-il? Est-ce cela ma vie? N'était-ce que cela? Est-ce que cela continuera ainsi, toujours?" A l'idée d'enfiler à perte de vue des semaines, des mois, des années que n'éclaireraient nulle attente, nulle promesse, j'eus le souffle coupé: on aurait dit que, sans prévenir, le monde était mort. Cette détresse non plus, je ne savais pas la nommer.

Pendant dix à quinze jours, je me traînai d'heure en heure, du jour au lendemain, les jambes molles. Un après-midi, je me déshabillais dans le vestiaire de l'institut, quand Zaza apparut. Nous nous sommes mises à parler, à raconter, à commenter; les mots se précipitaient sur mes lèvres, et dans ma poitrine tournoyaient mille soleils; dans un éblouissement de joie, je me suis dit: "C'est elle qui me manquait!" Si radicale était mon ignorance des vraies aventures du coeur que je n'avais pas songé à me dire: "Je souffre de son absence." Il me fallait sa présence pour réaliser le besoin que j'avais d'elle. Ce fut une évidence fulgurante. Brusquement, conventions, routines, clichés volèrent en éclats et je fus submergée par une émotion qui n'était prévue dans aucun code. Je me laissai soulever par cette joie qui déferlait en moi, violente et fraîche comme l'eau des cascades, nue comme un beau granit. Quelques jours plus tard, j'arrivai au cours en avance, et je regardai avec une espèce de stupeur le tabouret de Zaza: "Si elle ne devait plus jamais s'y asseoir, si elle mourait, que deviendrais-je?" Et de nouveau une évidence me foudroya: "Je ne peux plus vivre sans elle." C'était un peu effrayant: elle allait, venait, loin de moi, et tout mon bonheur, mon existence même reposaient entre ses mains. J'imaginai que Mademoiselle Gontran allait entrer, balayant le sol de sa longue jupe, et elle nous dirait: "Priez, mes enfants: votre petite compagne, Elizabeth Mabille, a été rappellée par Dieu la nuit dernière." Eh bien, me dis-je, je mourrais sur l'heure! Je glisserais de mon tabouret, et je tomberais sur le sol, expirante. Cette solution me rassura. Je ne croyais pas pour de bon qu'une grâce divine m'ôterait la vie; mais je ne redoutais pas non plus réellement la mort de Zaza. J'avais été jusqu'à m'avouer la dépendance où me mettait mon attachement pour elle: je n'osai pas en affronter toutes les conséquences.

Je ne réclamais pas que Zaza éprouvât à mon égard un sentiment aussi définitif: il me suffisait d'être sa camarade préférée. L'admiration que je lui vouais ne me dépréciait pas à mes propres yeux. L'amour n'est pas l'envie. Je ne concevais rien de mieux au monde que d'être moi-même, et d'aimer Zaza.

Mémoires d'une jeune fille rangée, pp. 94–95
Memoirs of a Dutiful Daughter, pp. 99–100

8. "Dans ma famille on a toujours été pour la primauté du spirituel."

"Marguerite," in "La Primauté du spirituel"

CHAPTER VI

1. A Vienne, les Juifs lavaient les trottoirs avec des acides qui leur rongeaient les doigts, sous les yeux amusés des passants; nous n'allions pas nous faire tuer pour ça; ni pour empêcher dans les nuits de Prague le sourd éclatement des suicides; ni pour prévenir ces incendies qui s'allumeraient bientôt dans les villages de Pologne. Tout occupés à déclarer pourquoi nous ne voulions pas mourir, nous inquiétons-nous de savoir pourquoi nous vivions encore.

> *Le Sang des autres*, p. 124
> *The Blood of Others*, p. 158

2. Nous n'avons pas oser tuer, nous n'avons pas voulu mourir, et cette vermine verte nous dévore vivants. Les femmes et les nouveaux-nés crèvent dans les fossés; sur ce sol qui n'est déjà plus le nôtre un immense réseau de fer s'est abattu, enserrant par millions les hommes de France. A cause de moi: chacun est responsable de tout. Une nuit, sous le piano, il griffait le tapis, et cette chose amère était dans sa gorge; mais il n'était qu'un enfant, il avait pleuré et dormi.

> *Le Sang des autres*, p. 173
> *The Blood of Others*, pp. 222–223

3. La femme restait immobile au milieu de la place. L'autobus démarra lourdement.

"Ruth! Ruth!" Elle tendit les mains en avant et partit en courant derrière la voiture. Elle portait des escarpins à talons hauts tout éculés, et elle courait par saccades maladroites. Un agent la suivait à grands pas d'homme, sans hâte. Elle cria encore: "Ruth!" un cri strident et sans espoir. Et puis elle s'arrêta au coin de la rue et mit la tête dans ses mains. La petite place était toute calme, et elle était là debout, au milieu du dimanche bleu, la tête dans ses mains, avec son coeur qui s'en allait en morceaux. L'agent mit la main sur son épaule.

"Ah! pourquoi? pourquoi?" pensa Hélène avec désespoir. Elle pleurait, mais elle demeurait immobile comme les autres, et elle regardait. Elle était là, et sa présence ne faisait aucune différence. Elle traversa la place. "Comme si je n'existais pas. Et pourtant j'existe. J'existe dans ma chambre fermée, j'existe dans le vide. Je ne compte pas. Est-ce que c'est ma faute?" Devant le Panthéon, des soldats allemands descendaient d'un car de tourisme; ils avaient l'air plutôt fatigués, ils ne ressemblaient pas à ces vainqueurs fringants qui criaient: "Heil!" sur les routes. "Je regardais passer l'Histoire, c'était mon histoire. Tout ça m'arrive à moi."

Le Sang des autres, p. 215
The Blood of Others, pp. 279–280

4. "Je n'ai plus peur." Elle se sentait légère et comblée comme aux plus beaux soirs de son enfance, quand elle reposait dans les bras d'un Dieu paternel. Etre mort: on n'*est* jamais mort. Il n'y a plus personne pour être mort. Je suis vivante. Je serai toujours vivante. Elle sentait sa vie qui battait dans sa poitrine et cet instant était éternel.

Le Sang des autres, p. 219
The Blood of Others, pp. 283–284

5. Nous pouvions nous jeter contre l'armée du duc, mettre le feu à nos maisons et mourir tous ensemble.

Les Bouches inutiles, p. 79

6. Une mort librement choisie n'est pas un mal. Mais ces femmes et ces vieillards que vous jetterez au fossé, aucun choix ne leur est permis. Et vous leur volerez leur mort avec leur vie. Nous ne ferons pas cela! Que cette nuit, uni dans une seule volonté, un peuple libre affronte son destin.

Ibid., pp. 132–133

7. "Nos bourreaux nous ont fait de bien mauvaises moeurs" écrivait avec regret Gracchus Babeuf. Nous aussi, sous l'oppression nazie en face des traîtres qui s'en faisaient les complices, nous avons vu éclore dans nos coeurs des sentiments vénéneux dont jamais nous n'avions pressenti le goût. . . .

Depuis juin 1940 nous avons appris la colère et la haine. Nous avons souhaité l'humiliation et la mort de nos ennemis. Et aujourd'hui, chaque fois qu'un tribunal condamne un criminel de guerre, un dénonciateur, un collaborationiste, nous nous sentons responsable de son verdict. . . . Nous nous sommes félicités de la mort de Mussolini, de la pendaison des bourreaux de Kharkov, des larmes de Darnand: par là même nous avons participé à leur condamnation. Leurs crimes nous avaient atteints au coeur de nous-mêmes; ce sont nos valeurs, nos raisons de vivre, qui s'affirment par leur châtiment.

"Oeil pour oeil," in *L'Existentialisme et la sagesse des nations*,
pp. 125–127

8. Un soldat qui tue en combattant n'est pas haïssable parce qu'il obéit à des consignes et parce qu'il y a réciprocité de situation entre son adversaire et lui; ni la mort, ni la souffrance, ni la captivité ne sont en soi des scandales. Il n'y a scandale que du moment où un homme traite ses semblables comme des objets, où il leur dénie par les tortures, l'humiliation, la servitude, l'assassinat, leur existence d'hommes.

Ibid., p. 133

9. La mort d'Hitler nous a frustrés; on souhaiterait qu'il fût vivant pour se rendre compte de sa ruine, pour "comprendre." La vengeance idéale, c'est celle que Louis XI tira de La Balue, celle que Judex tire du méchant banquier qu'il enferme pour la vie dans une cellule: voilà la conscience présente et captive de la situation qu'on lui impose, on la fige dans le désespoir; encore n'est-il pas sûr qu'elle ne finira pas par s'évader dans la folie.

Ibid., pp. 139–140

10. Et dans son box, seul, coupé de tous, il y avait un homme que les circonstances portaient au plus haut de lui-même: cet homme était mis en présence de sa mort et par là de toute sa vie qu'il lui fallait assumer devant la mort; quelle que fût cette vie, quelles que fussent les raisons de sa mort, la dignité avec laquelle il se comportait en cette situation extrême exigeait notre respect dans le moment où nous aurions le plus souhaité le mépriser. Nous désirions la mort du rédacteur de *Je suis partout*, non celle de cet homme tout appliqué à bien mourir.

Ibid., p. 149

11. C'est fête cette nuit: le premier Noël de paix; le dernier Noël à Buchenwald; le dernier Noël sur terre, le premier Noël que Diego n'a pas vécu. Nous dansions, nous nous embrassions autour de l'arbre scintillant de promesses, et ils étaient nombreux, ah! si nombreux à ne pas être là! Personne n'avait recueilli leurs dernières paroles et ils n'étaient enterrés nulle part: le vide les avait engloutis. Deux jours après la libération Geneviève avait touché un cercueil: était-ce bien le bon? On n'avait pas retrouvé le corps de Jacques; un camarade prétendait qu'il avait enterré des carnets sous un arbre: quels carnets? quel arbre? Sonia avait fait demander un pullover et des bas de soie, et puis elle n'avait plus jamais rien demandé. Où étaient les os de Rachel et ceux de la très belle Rosa? Dans ses bras que tant de fois avaient étreint le doux corps de Rose, Lambert serrait Nadine, et Nadine riait

comme au temps où Diego la serrait dans ses bras. Je regardais l'allée de sapins au fond des grands miroirs, et je pensais: Voici les bougies, le houx, le gui qu'ils ne voient pas; tout ce qui m'est donné je leur vole. "On les a abattus." Qui le premier: son père ou lui? la mort n'entrait pas dans ses plans: a-t-il su qu'il allait mourir? s'est-il révolté, résigné? comment savoir? et maintenant qu'il est mort, quelle importance? . . . Les morts sont morts; pour eux, il n'y a pas de problèmes: mais nous les vivants, après cette nuit de fête, nous allons nous réveiller; et alors comment vivrons-nous?

Les Mandarins, pp. 27–30
The Mandarins, pp. 32–35

12. Je fus bouleversée et par l'égarement de Lise et pour mon compte; bien des morts déjà m'avaient revoltée, mais celle-ci m'atteignait intimement. Bourla avait vécu tout près de moi, je l'avais adopté dans mon coeur, et il n'avait que dix-neuf ans. Sartre tentait pieusement de me convaincre qu'en un sens toute vie est achevée, qu'il n'est pas plus absurde de mourir à dix-neuf ans qu'à quatre-vingts: je ne le croyais pas . . . pas de tombe, pas de cadavre, pas un os. Comme si rien, absolument, n'avait eu lieu. . . . Ce néant m'égarait. . . . Il n'avait pas choisi d'affronter la mort, elle avait fondu sur lui sans son consentement: l'avait-il pendant un instant vue face à face? Qui avait-on abattu le premier: son père ou lui? S'il avait su, j'en étais sure, tout haut ou en silence il avait crié *non,* et cet affreux soubresaut restait à jamais et vainement figé dans l'éternité. Il avait crié non et plus rien n'avait été. Je ne trouvais pas cette histoire supportable. Mais je la supportai. . . . Depuis quelques mois il m'avait semblé ressusciter, la vie à nouveau m'éblouissait; et voilà que Bourla disparaissait: jamais je n'avais touché avec une telle évidence la capricieuse horreur de notre condition mortelle. . . . à cause de sa mort même, et de tout de qu'elle signifiait, les moments où je me donnai au scandale, au désespoir prirent une intensité que je n'avais jamais connue: vraiment infernale. Mais dès que je m'en échappais, de nouveau j'étais happée par les splendeurs de l'avenir, et par tout ce qui composait au jour le jour mon bonheur.

La Force de l'âge, pp. 592–593
The Prime of Life, pp. 457–458

13. Et par le fait, s'il est vrai que les hommes cherchent dans l'avenir une garantie de leur réussite, une négation de leurs échecs,

il est vrai qu'ils éprouvent aussi le besoin de nier la fuite indéfinie du temps et de tenir leur présent entre leurs mains. Il faut affirmer l'existence au présent si l'on ne veut pas que la vie tout entière se définisse comme un échappement vers le néant. C'est ainsi que les sociétés instituent des fêtes dont le rôle est d'arrêter le mouvement de la transcendance, de poser la fin comme fin. Les heures qui suivirent la libération de Paris, par exemple, furent une immense fête collective exaltant la fin heureuse et absolue de cette histoire singulière qui était précisément l'occupation de Paris. . . . Un des rôles de l'art, c'est de fixer d'une manière plus durable cette affirmation passionnée de l'existence: la fête est à l'origine du théâtre, de la musique, de la danse, de la poésie. En racontant une histoire, en la représentant, on la fait exister dans sa singularité avec son commencement, sa fin, sa gloire ou sa honte. Et c'est ainsi en vérité qu'il faut la vivre. Dans la fête, dans l'art, les hommes expriment leur besoin de se sentir vivre absolument. Ils doivent accomplir réellement ce voeu. Ce qui les arrête, c'est que, dès qu'ils donnent au mot fin son double sens de but et d'achève-ment, ils aperçoivent clairement cette ambiguïté de leur condition, qui est la plus fondamentale de toutes: que tout mouvement vivant est un glissement vers la mort. Mais s'ils acceptent de l'envisager en face, ils découvrent aussi que tout mouvement vers la mort est vie. On criait autrefois: "Le roi est mort, vive le roi"; ainsi il faut que le présent meure afin qu'il vive; l'existence ne doit pas nier cette mort qu'elle porte en son coeur, mais la vouloir; elle doit s'affirmer comme absolu dans sa finitude même; c'est au sein du transitoire que l'homme s'accomplit, ou jamais. Il lui faut regarder ses entreprises comme finies et les vouloir absolument.

Pour une morale de l'ambiguïté, pp. 175–178
The Ethics of Ambiguity, pp. 125–127

14. Both of these expressions are used and developed by Edgar Morin in *L'Homme et la mort* (Paris: Buchet-Castel, Éditions Corrêa, 1951).

15. Sartre pensait beaucoup à l'après-guerre; il était bien décidé à ne plus se tenir à l'écart de la vie politique. Sa nouvelle morale, basée sur la notion d'authenticité, et qu'il s'efforçait à mettre en pratique exigeait que l'homme "assumait" sa "situation"; et la seule manière de le faire c'était de la dépasser en s'engageant dans une action: toute autre attitude était une fuite, une prétention vide, une mascarade fondées sur la mauvaise foi. On voit qu'un

sérieux changement s'était produit en lui, et aussi en moi qui me
ralliais tout de suite à son idée; car notre premier soin naguère
avait été de tenir notre situation à distance par des jeux, des
leurres, des mensonges.

La Force de l'âge, p. 442
The Prime of Life, p. 342

16. . . . À la fin de juin [1944] des "météores" s'abattirent sur
Londres; ils tombaient capricieusement, sans qu'aucun signal les
annonçât; à n'importe quel instant on pouvait imaginer que
quelqu'un qu'on aimait venait d'être tué; cette insécurité diffuse
me paraissait la pire des épreuves, je redoutais d'avoir un jour à
l'affronter.

Pour l'instant nous l'ignorons. Nous nous promenions, nous
prenions des verres, nous causions.

La Force de l'âge, p. 600
The Prime of Life, p. 463

17. . . . On peut vivre avec une grande douceur un présent
tout entouré de menaces.

La Force de l'âge, p. 406
The Prime of Life, p. 314

18. . . . Nous ne voulions pas manquer les journées de la
libération.

La Force de l'âge, p. 605
The Prime of Life, p. 466

19. Jusqu'à la guerre, j'avais suivi ma pente; j'apprenais le monde
et je me construisais un bonheur: la morale se confondait avec
cette pratique; c'était un âge d'or. . . . A partir de 1939, tout
changea; le monde devint un chaos, et je cessai de rien bâtir; je
n'eus d'autre recours que cette conjuration verbale: une morale
abstraite; je cherchai des raisons, des formules pour me justifier de
subir ce qui m'était imposé. J'en trouvai auxquelles je crois encore; je découvris la solidarité, mes responsabilités, et la possibilité
de consentir à la mort pour que la vie gardât un sens. Mais j'appris
ces vérités en quelque sorte contre moi-même; j'usai de mots
pour m'exhorter à les accueillir; je m'expliquais, je me persuadais,
je me faisais la leçon; c'est cette leçon que je m'efforçai de trans-
mettre, sans me rendre compte qu'elle n'avait pas forcément la
même fraîcheur pour le lecteur que pour moi.

La Force de l'âge, p. 561
The Prime of Life, pp. 432–433

20. Fêtes nocturnes des amours naissantes, fêtes massives des jours de victoire: il y a toujours un goût mortel au fond des ivresses vivantes, mais la mort, pendant un moment fulgurant, est réduite à rien.

La Force de l'âge, p. 588
The Prime of Life, p. 453

21. Mais dans l'ensemble, une des constantes de cette littérature, c'est l'ennui; elle ôte à la vie son sel, son feu: son élan vers l'avenir. Sartre définissait la littérature comme une fête: funèbre ou joyeuse, mais une fête: nous en voilà bien loin! C'est un univers mort que construisent les disciples de la nouvelle école.

La Force des choses, p. 649
Force of Circumstance, p. 622

22. Il est bien rare qu'on coïncide exactement avec une joie longtemps attendue: cette chance m'était donnée.

La Force de l'âge, p. 611
The Prime of Life, p. 471

23. La mort devenait une présence quotidienne, impossible de penser à rien d'autre.

La Force de l'âge, p. 449
The Prime of Life, p. 347

24. Jamais ma mort et la mort des autres ne m'occupèrent d'une façon aussi pressante que pendant ces années.

La Force de l'âge, p. 615
The Prime of Life, p. 474

25. . . . En dépit de toutes ces morts derrière moi, de mes indignations, de mes révoltes, je me rétablissais dans le bonheur; tant de coups reçus: aucun ne m'avait fracassée. Je survivais, et même j'étais indemne.

La Force de l'âge, p. 615
The Prime of Life, p. 474

CHAPTER VII

1. . . . À travers la jouissance maniaque de Xavière, à travers sa haine et sa jalousie, le scandale éclatait, aussi monstrueux, aussi définitif que la mort; en face de Françoise, et cependant sans elle, quelque chose existait comme une condamnation sans recours:

libre, absolue, irréductible, une conscience étrangère se dressait.
. . . Des images traversèrent Françoise: un vieux veston, une
clairière abandonnée, un coin du Pôle Nord où Pierre et Xavière
vivaient loin d'elle un mystérieux tête-à-tête. Déjà il lui était arrivé
de sentir comme ce soir son être se dissoudre au profit d'êtres
inaccessibles, mais jamais elle n'avait réalisé avec une lucidité si
parfaite son propre anéantissement.

L'Invitée, pp. 318–319
She Came to Stay, pp. 291–292

2. Vassieux, Hiroshima. En un an on avait fait du chemin. Ça
se donnerait la prochaine guerre. Et l'après-guerre donc: elle serait
encore plus soignée que celle-ci. A moins qu'il n'y ait pas d'après-
guerre. A moins que le vaincu ne s'amuse à faire sauter le globe.
Ça se pourrait très bien. Il ne se casserait pas en morceaux, ad-
mettons, il continuerait à tourner sur lui-même, glacé, désert: ce
n'était pas plus réjouissant à imaginer. L'idée de la mort n'avait
jamais gêné Henri; mais soudain ce silence lunaire l'épouvantait:
il n'y aurait plus d'hommes! En face de cette éternité sourde-
muette à quoi ça rimait-il d'aligner les mots, de tenir des meetings? On n'avait qu'à attendre en silence le cataclysme universel,
ou sa petite mort personnelle. Rien n'était rien.

Les Mandarins, pp. 229–230
The Mandarins, p. 248

3. "Maman, pourquoi est-ce qu'on existe?" . . . Quelle anxiété
dans les yeux de cette petite fille que je traite encore comme un
bébé. Pourquoi se pose-t-elle cette question? Voilà donc ce qui
la fait pleurer. . . .
"Mais les gens qui ne sont pas heureux, pourquoi est-ce qu'ils
existent?"
"Tu as vu des gens malheureux? Où ça, mon chéri? . . . On
peut soigner les malades, donner de l'argent aux pauvres, on peut
un tas de choses. . . ."
"Tu crois? pour tout le monde?"
"Tu penses que je pleurerai toute la journée s'il y avait des gens
dont les malheurs soient sans remède. Tu me raconteras tout. Et
je te promets que nous trouverons des remèdes. Je te promets,"
répète-t-elle en caressant les cheveux de Catherine. "Dors maintenant, ma petite chérie."

Les Belles Images, pp. 29–30
Les Belles Images, pp. 29–30

4. Ma première rencontre avec la mort, comme j'ai pleuré. Ensuite j'ai pleuré de moins en moins: mes parents, mon beau-frère, mon beau-père, les amis. C'est ça aussi, vieillir. Tant de morts derrière soi, regrettés, oubliés.

"L'Age de discrétion," in *La Femme rompue*, p. 73

5. Elle [sa fille] est morte et alors? Les morts ne sont pas des saints. . . . L'affreux souvenir le ciel bleu toutes ces fleurs Albert en larmes devant tout le monde on se tient bon Dieu. Moi je me suis tenue et pourtant je savais que ce coup-là je ne m'en relèverais jamais. C'était moi qu'on enterrait. Je suis enterrée.

"Monologue," in *La Femme rompue*, pp. 97–99

6. (Peut-être la mort de mon père n'est-elle pas étrangère à ce laisser-aller. Quelque chose s'est brisé. J'ai arrêté le temps à partir de ce moment-là.)

"La Femme rompue," in *La Femme rompue*, p. 210

7. C'était sa volonté qui était en train de s'accomplir, plus rien ne la séparait d'elle-même. Elle avait enfin choisie. Elle s'était choisie.

L'Invitée, p. 441
She Came to Stay, p. 404

8. Tu m'as donné le courage d'accepter à jamais le risque et l'angoisse, de supporter mes crimes et le remords, qui me déchirera sans fin. Il n'y a pas d'autre route.

Le Sang des autres, p. 224
The Blood of Others, p. 292

9. Je ne veux pas être un brin d'herbe.

Tous les Hommes sont mortels, p. 16

10. . . . Jamais je ne serais un autre.

Ibid., p. 289

11. Ce fut quand l'heure commença de sonner au clocher qu'elle poussa le premier cri.

Ibid., p. 359

12. . . . Les belles images demeurant intactes en dépit de toutes les désillusions.

Les Belles Images, p. 237
Les Belles Images, p. 207

CHAPTER VIII

1. On ne parle pas volontiers de la mort en Amérique; jamais on ne croise un enterrement dans les rues. . . . Quant à moi, ces *Home* avenants qui s'ouvrent entre un *drug-store* et un bar me font frissonner; je m'attends toujours à voir quelque *zombie*, quelque vampire s'en échapper; c'est que la vérité de la mort y est vraiment niée; dans les cimetières elle se révèle et c'est ce qui donne à ces jardins de deuil leur charme inattendu. Soudain, dans ce pays où le bonheur et la santé sont garantis par les procédés les plus modernes, il se découvre que les hommes meurent. . . . Les cimetières rappellent que chaque existence est singulière et chaque homme à soi seul un absolu. . . . Ce sont les tombes qui, en Amérique, affirment avec le plus d'autorité que l'homme est encore humain. . . . Leurs cimetières ont plus de personnalité que leurs villes. Parmi ces dalles à demi enfoncés dans la terre, on s'évade enfin de la banalité quotidienne.

L'Amérique au jour le jour, p. 82

2. S'il me disait un jour: "Rendez-vous, dans vingt-deux mois exactement, à 17 heures, sur l'Acropole" je serais assurée de le retrouver sur l'Acropole, à 17 heures exactement, vingt-deux mois plus tard. D'une manière plus générale, je savais qu'aucun malheur ne me viendrait jamais par lui, à moins qu'il ne mourût avant moi.

La Force de l'âge, p. 28
The Prime of Life, p. 24

3. Je raccrochai, mais je ne retrouvai pas la paix; cette alerte avait un tout autre sens que celle de 1940; alors c'étaient des dangers extérieurs qui menaçaient Sartre; soudain je réalisai que, comme tout le monde, il portait sa mort en lui. Je ne l'avais jamais regardée en face; contre elle j'invoquai mon propre anéantissement qui tout en m'épouvantant me rassurait; mais en cet instant j'étais hors jeu; peu importait que je me trouve ou non sur cette terre le jour où il disparaîtrait, que je lui survive ou non: ce jour viendrait. Dans vingt ans ou demain c'était la même imminence: il mourra. Quel noir éblouissement! La crise se dénoua. Mais quelque chose d'irréversible était arrivé; la mort m'avait saisie; elle n'était plus un scandale métaphysique, mais une qualité de nos artères; non plus un manchon de nuit autour de nous, mais une présence intime

qui pénétrait ma vie, altérant les goûts, les odeurs, les lumières, les souvenirs, les projets: tout.

La Force des choses, p. 320
Force of Circumstance, p. 306

4. Mardi 14. Vraiment assez horribles journées. Dans cet avion qui avait perdu un moteur, à six heures de Shannon, c'était ainsi: une peur constante, avec de brefs répits et le réveil de la peur. De même avec Sartre. Par moments il semble mieux; ou, comme hier, il embrouille ses mots, il marche avec peine, son écriture, son orthographe sont affolantes, et je m'affole. Le ventricule gauche assez fatigué, dit le médecin. Il faudrait le vrai repos qu'il ne prendra pas. Notre mort est en nous, non pas comme le noyau dans le fruit, comme le sens de notre vie; en nous, mais étrangère, ennemie, affreuse. Rien d'autre ne compte. Mon livre, les critiques, les lettres, les gens qui m'en parlent, tout ce qui m'aurait fait plaisir, radicalement annulé. Je n'ai même plus le courage de tenir ce journal. . . . Je vois que je vais arrêter ce journal. . . . J'ai mis les feuilles dans une chemise sur laquelle j'ai écrit, impulsivement: *Journal d'une défaite*. Et je n'y ai plus touché. . . . Un peu plus tard, causant avec un très ancien ami, Herbaud, je dis que, somme toute, nous n'avions plus rien à attendre sinon notre mort et celle de nos proches. Qui s'en ira le premier? Qui survivra? Voilà maintenant les questions que je posais à l'avenir: "Allez, allez, me dit-il, nous n'en sommes pas là: vous avez toujours été en avance pour votre âge. "Je ne me trompais pas pourtant . . ."

La Force des choses, pp. 473–477
Force of Circumstance, pp. 451–454

5. La seule chose à la fois neuve et importante qui puisse m'arriver, c'est le malheur. Ou je verrai Sartre mort, ou je mourrai avant lui. C'est affreux de ne pas être là pour consoler quelqu'un de la peine qu'on lui fait en le quittant; c'est affreux qu'il vous abandonne et se taise. A moins de la plus improbable des chances, un de ces lots sera le mien. Parfois je souhaite en finir vite afin d'abréger cette angoisse.

La Force des choses, p. 686
Force of Circumstance, p. 657

6. Il [Nizan] nous intéressa surtout quand il aborda un thème qui entre tous lui tenait au coeur: la mort. Bien qu'il n'y fît jamais

allusion, nous savions dans quelle angoisse il pouvait tomber à l'idée de disparaître un jour, pour toujours; il lui arrivait d'errer pendant des journées, buvant de zinc en zinc de grands verres de vin rouge, pour fuir cette terreur. Il s'était demandé si la foi socialiste aidait à la conjurer. Il l'espérait et il avait longuement interrogé à ce propos les jeunes Soviétiques: tous avaient répondu qu'en face de la mort la camaraderie, la solidarité n'étaient d'aucun secours, et qu'ils en avaient peur. Officiellement, par exemple quand il rendait compte de son voyage au cours d'un meeting, Nizan interprétait le fait de façon optimiste; au fur et à mesure que les problèmes techniques se résolvaient expliquait-il, l'amour et la mort retrouvaient en U.R.S.S. toute leur importance: un nouvel humanisme était en train de naître. Mais causant avec nous, il s'exprima tout autrement. Ça lui avait porté un coup de découvrir que, là-bas comme ici, chacun mourait seul et le savait.

La Force de l'âge, p. 213
The Prime of Life, p. 166

7. . . . . Nizan avait été tué; on ne savait pas exactement où ni comment, mais le fait était certain. Sa femme et ses enfants avaient passé en Amérique. J'en eus le coeur retourné. Nizan qui détestait tant la morte: s'était-il vu mourir?

La Force de l'âge, p. 480
The Prime of Life, p. 371

8. Elle [Hélène] ne revit pas mon père qui mourut au mois de juillet. Il avait été opéré de la prostate et on avait pu croire d'abord qu'il avait bien réagi. Mais il avait été affaibli par des mois de sous-alimentation, et surtout par le choc de la défaite et de l'occupation: la tuberculose des vieillards l'emporta en quelques jours. Il accueillit la mort avec une indifférence qui m'étonna; il avait souvent dit qu'il lui importait peu qu'elle survînt un jour plutôt qu'un autre, puisque de toute façon on ne lui échappait pas; d'ailleurs, il ne lui restait guère de raisons de vivre, en ce monde auquel il n'entendait rien; il n'empêche: j'admirai qu'il retournât si paisiblement au néant; il ne se leurrait pas puisqu'il me demanda si je pouvais, sans peiner ma mère, éviter qu'aucun prêtre ne vînt à son chevet: elle se conforma à ce désir. J'assistai à son agonie, à ce dur travail vivant par lequel la vie s'abolit, m'essayant vaine-ment à capter le mystère de ce départ vers nulle part. Je restai longtemps seule avec lui après le sursaut final; d'abord, il fut mort

mais présent: c'était lui. Et puis je le vis s'éloigner vertigineuse-
ment de moi: je me retrouvai penchée sur un cadavre.

La Force de l'âge, p. 503
The Prime of Life, p. 389

9. Dans ces débats, Jouvet ne prenait pas parti: pratiquement,
il était mort; le coeur malade, se sachant plus ou moins condamné
il s'était fait photographier, le mercredi saint, en train de recevoir
les Cendres. Il détestait les blasphèmes de Sartre. Le pouce droit
rivé sur son pouls gauche, le regard sur sa montre, sous prétexte
de minuter les scènes il les laissait filer sans une observation.

La Force des choses, p. 259
Force of Circumstance, p. 240

10. Depuis des années, je faisais taper mes textes par Lucienne
Baudin, une femme de mon âge, agréable; elle avait une petite fille,
d'une dizaine d'années. En dépit de quelques aventures masculines,
ses goûts la portaient vers les femmes; elle vivait avec une quin-
quagénaire; elles élevaient l'enfant ensemble. Elle me parlait de
ses problèmes, de ses ennuis d'argent, de ses amitiés, de ses
amours, et de ce monde moins connu que celui des pédérastes: les
lesbiennes. Je la voyais peu mais avec sympathie. Au bout d'un
certain temps elle se mit à faire son travail très mal et sans
ponctualité; elle devint nerveuse: Je crois que j'ai quelque chose
au sein me dit-elle. Je la pressai de voir un médecin: Je ne peux
pas m'arrêter de travailler. Un an plus tard elle me dit: J'ai un
cancer: c'est déjà gros comme une noix. On l'envoya à l'Institut
du cancer à Villejuif; j'allai la voir et à mon arrivée elle fondit en
larmes; elle partageait sa chambre avec trois autres malades, l'une
à qui on venait d'ôter un sein, hurlait de douleur entre les piqûres
de morphine; une autre, le sein droit enlevé quelques années plus
tôt, avait maintenant le sein gauche pris. Lucienne était terrorisée.
Il était trop tard pour l'opérer, on la soignait avec des rayons. Les
rayons ne réussirent pas. On la renvoya chez elle et on lui injecta
des hormones mâles. Quand je retournai la voir, je la reconnus à
peine: son visage était gonflé, une moustache ombrageait ses lèvres,
elle parlait avec une voix d'homme; seul restait intact l'éclat de
ses dents blanches. De temps en temps, elle portait la main à sa
poitrine enveloppée de bandelettes et elle gémissait: on devinait
fragile et douloureux, ce paquet de glandes où la pourriture s'était
mise et j'aurais voulu fuir. Elle pleurait. Elle écrivait à des guéris-
seurs, elle essayait des drogues miracle, elle rêvait d'aller en

Amérique consulter des spécialistes. Et elle pleurait. On la con-
duisit à l'hôpital: dans les lits voisins de vieilles femmes se
mouraient du cancer. On continua les injections d'hormones.
Boursouflée, barbue, ridiculement hideuse, elle souffrait et elle ne
se résignait pas à sa mort. Quand je rentrai de Saint-Tropez, son
amie me dit qu'elle agonisait; le lendemain elle était morte, après
s'être débattue vingt-quatre heures. Elle a l'air d'une vieillarde de
quatre-vingts ans, me dit son amie. Je n'eus pas le courage d'aller
regarder son cadavre.

> *La Force des choses*, pp. 263–264
> *Force of Circumstance*, pp. 244–245

11. J'accueillis avec un certain plaisir la mort du pape, celle de
Foster Dulles.

> *La Force des choses*, p. 485
> *Force of Circumstance*, p. 462

12. A peu de temps de là—dix ans exactement après que les
médecins lui aient dit: Vous en avez pour dix ans,—Boris Vian
mourut d'irritation et d'une crise cardiaque, pendant une projection privée du film *J'irai cracher sur vos tombes*. Arrivant chez
Sartre, au début de l'après-midi, je dépliai *Le Monde* et j'appris la
nouvelle. Je l'avais vu pour la dernière fois aux *Trois Baudets*.
Nous avions bu un verre: il n'avait guère changé depuis notre
première conversation. J'avais eu beaucoup d'affection pour lui.
Pourtant, c'est seulement quelques jours plus tard, en voyant dans
Match la photo d'une civière recouverte d'une étoffe que j'ai
réalisé: sous l'étoffe, c'est Vian. Et j'ai compris que si rien en
moi ne se révoltait, c'est que j'étais habituée déjà à ma propre
mort.

> *La Force des choses*, pp. 490–491
> *Force of Circumstance*, p. 467

13. J'étais seule chez Sartre, un après-midi de janvier, quand le
téléphone sonna: Camus s'est tué tout à l'heure en auto, me dit
Lanzmann. Il rentrait du Midi avec un ami, la voiture s'était
fracassée contre un platane, et il était mort sur le coup. Je reposai
l'écouteur. La gorge serrée, la bouche tremblante: Je ne vais pas
me mettre à pleurer, me dis-je. Il n'était plus rien pour moi.
Je restai debout contre la fenêtre, regardant descendre la nuit
sur Saint-Germain-des-Prés, incapable de me calmer comme de
sombrer dans un vrai chagrin. Sartre fut ému, lui aussi, et toute

la soirée avec Bost nous avons parlé de Camus. Avant de me coucher, j'ai avalé du belladénal; depuis la guérison de Sartre, je n'en usais plus, j'aurais dû m'endormir; je ne fermai pas l'oeil. Je me suis levée, vêtue à la diable, et je suis partie marcher dans la nuit. Ce n'était pas l'homme de cinquante ans que je regrettais; ce n'était pas ce juste sans justice, à la morgue ombrageuse et sévèrement masqué, qu'avait rayé de mon coeur son consentement aux crimes de la France; c'était le compagnon des années d'espoir, dont le visage nu riait et souriait si bien, le jeune écrivain ambitieux, fou de la vie, de ses plaisirs, de ses triomphes, de la camaraderie, de l'amitié, de l'amour, du bonheur. La mort le ressuscitait; pour lui le tempts n'existait plus, hier n'avait pas plus de vérité qu'avant-hier; Camus, tel que je l'avais aimé surgissait de la nuit, au même moment retrouvé et douloureusement perdu. Toujours quand meurt un homme, meurt un enfant, un adolescent, un jeune homme: chacun pleure celui qui lui a été cher. Il tombait une pluie fine et froide; sur l'avenue d'Orléans, des clochards dormaient dans l'embrasure des portes, recroquevillés et transis. Tout me déchirait: cette misère, ce malheur, cette ville, le monde, et la vie, et la mort.

Au réveil, j'ai pensé: Cette matinée, il ne la voit pas. Ce n'était pas la première fois que je me disais ça; mais chaque fois est la première. Cayatte est venu, je me rappelle, nous avons discuté le scénario; cette conversation n'était qu'un simulacre; loin d'avoir quitté le monde, Camus, par la violence de l'événement qui l'avait frappé, en était devenu le centre et je ne voyais plus que par ses yeux éteints; j'étais passée du côté où il n'y a rien et je constatais, stupide et navrée, les choses qui continuaient d'être alors que je n'y étais plus; tout le jour, je chancelai au bord de l'impossible expérience: toucher l'envers de ma propre absence.

Ce soir-là, j'avais projeté de revoir *Citizen Kane;* j'arrivai en avance au cinéma et je m'assis dans le café d'en face, avenue de l'Opéra. Des gens lisaient les journaux, indifférents au gros titre de la première page et à la photo qui m'aveuglait. Je pensais à la femme qui aimait Camus, au supplice de rencontrer à tous les coins de rue ce visage public, qui semblait appartenir à tous autant qu'à elle et qui n'avait plus de bouche pour lui dire le contraire. Ça me semblait un raffinement, des fanfares qui clament au vent votre secret désespoir. Michel Gallimard avait été grièvement blessé; il avait été mêlé à nos fêtes en 44 et 45; il mourut lui aussi. Vian, Camus, Michel: la série des morts avait commencé, elle continuerait jusqu'à la mienne, qui viendrait forcément trop tôt ou trop tard.

La Force des choses, pp. 508–509
Force of Circumstance, pp. 484–485

14. Au début de l'hiver Richard Wright avait brusquement succombé à une attaque au coeur. J'avais découvert New York avec lui, je gardais de lui quantité d'images précieuses qu'en un instant le néant me faucha. A Antibes, un coup de téléphone m'apprit la mort de Merleau-Ponty: pour lui aussi, soudain, un arrêt du coeur. Cette histoire qui m'arrive n'est plus la mienne ai-je pensé. Je n'imaginais certes plus que je me la racontais à ma guise, mais je croyais encore contribuer à la bâtir; en vérité elle m'échappait. J'assistais, impuissante, au jeu de forces étrangères: l'histoire, le temps, la mort. Cette fatalité ne me laissait même plus la consolation de pleurer. Regrets, révoltes, je les avais épuisés, j'étais vaincue, je lâchai prise. Hostile à cette société à laquelle j'appartenais, bannie, par l'âge, de l'avenir, dépouillée fibre par fibre du passé, je me réduisais à ma présence nue. Quelle glace!

La Force des choses, pp. 614–615
Force of Circumstance, p. 587

15. Un drame lointain acheva d'assombrir pour moi ce sombre automne. Au début d'octobre, Fanon avait eu une rechute et ses amis l'avaient envoyé se faire soigner aux U.S.A.: malgré sa répugnance, il avait accepté. Il s'était arrêté à Rome et Sartre avait passé quelques heures, dans sa chambre d'hôtel, en compagnie de Boulahrouf, le représentant du G.P.R.A. en Italie. Fanon gisait à plat sur son lit, si épuisé que pendant toute l'entrevue il n'ouvrit pas la bouche; le visage crispé, il bougeait sans cesse, réduit à une passivité contre laquelle tout son corps se révoltait.

A mon retour à Paris, Lanzmann me montra des lettres et des dépêches de la femme de Fanon. Celui-ci avait cru qu'en tant que membre du G.P.R.A. [Gouvernement provisoire de la république algérienne] il serait chaleureusement reçu à Washington: on l'avait abandonné dix jours, seul, sans soins, dans une chambre d'hôtel. Elle était venue le rejoindre, avec leur fils de six ans. Enfin transporté à l'hôpital, Fanon venait d'être opéré; on avait changé tout son sang, on espérait que le choc réveillerait sa moelle, mais il n'y avait aucun espoir de guérison; au mieux, il survivrait un an. Elle écrivit de nouveau, elle téléphona: à 6000 kilomètres de distance, nous suivîmes, au jour le jour cette agonie. Le livre de Fanon parut, il y eut des articles qui le couvrirent d'éloges; sa femme lui lut ceux de *L'Express* et de *L'Observateur*: "Ce n'est pas ça qui me rendra ma moelle," dit-il. Une nuit, à deux heures, elle téléphona à Lanzmann: Franz est mort, il avait succombé à une double pneumonie. A travers la sobriété de ses lettres on la sentait désespérée et Lanzmann, bien que la connaissant très peu, prit l'avion pour Washington. Il revint au bout de quelques jours, ahuri et secoué. Minute par minute Fanon avait vécu sa mort et l'avait sauvagement refusée; son agressivité ombrageuse s'était libérée dans ses délires de moribond; il détestait les Américains, ces racistes, et se méfiait de tout le personnel de l'hôpital; en s'éveillant, le dernier matin, il avait dit à sa femme, trahissant ses obsessions: "Cette nuit, ils m'ont mis dans la machine à laver." Son fils était entré dans sa chambre un jour où on lui faisait une transfusion; des tuyaux le rattachaient à des ballons en plastique remplis les uns de globules rouges, d'autres de globules blancs et de plaquettes; l'enfant sortit en hurlant: Les brigands! ils ont coupé mon père en morceaux. Dans les rues de Washington, il agitait d'un air provocant le drapeau vert et blanc. Les Algériens envoyèrent un avion spécial pour ramener le corps de Fanon à Tunis. On l'enterra en Algérie, dans un cimetière de l'A.L.N. [Armée de libération nationale]: pour la première fois et en pleine guerre les Algériens firent à l'un des leurs des funérailles nationales. Pendant une ou deux semaines, dans les rues de Paris, je rencontrai partout la photo de Fanon: dans les kiosques sur la couverture de *Jeune Afrique*, à la devanture de la librairie Maspero, plus jeune, plus calme que je ne l'avais vu, et très beau. Sa mort pesait lourd parce qu'il l'avait chargée de toute l'intensité de sa vie.

La Force des choses, pp. 633–635
Force of Circumstance, pp. 606–607

16. . . . Soudain, l'enfer remonta sur la terre. Marie-Claude Radziewski lui avait communiqué un dossier sur les traitements infligés par les harkis, dans les caves de la Goutte-d'Or, à des Musulmans que leur livrait la D.S.T. [Direction de la Surveillance du Territoire]: gégène, brûlures, empalements sur des bouteilles, pendaisons, étranglements, les tortures étaient entrecoupées d'action psychologique. Lanzmann écrivit là-dessus un article pour *Les Temps Modernes* et publia le dossier des plaintes. Une étu-

diante me raconta qu'elle avait vu de ses yeux, rue de la Goutte-d'Or, des hommes en sang que des harkis traînaient d'une maison à une autre. Les gens du quartier entendaient toutes les nuits des hurlements. Pourquoi? Pourquoi? Pourquoi?: ce cri indéfiniment répété d'un petit Algérien de quinze ans qui avait vu torturer toute sa famille * me déchirait les tympans et la gorge. Qu'elles étaient bénignes les révoltes où me jetaient jadis la condition humaine et l'idée abstraite de la mort! Contre la fatalité, on peut convulsivement se débattre, mais elle décourage la colère. Et du moins le scandale demeurait hors de moi. Aujourd'hui j'étais devenue scandale à mes propres yeux. Pourquoi? Pourquoi? Pourquoi devais-je me réveiller chaque matin dans la douleur et la rage, atteinte jusqu'aux moelles par un mal auquel je ne consentais pas et que je n'avais aucun moyen de conjurer? De toute façon, la vieillesse est une épreuve, la moins méritée, pensait Kant, la plus imprévue, disait Trotsky: mais qu'elle fit basculer dans l'ignominie une existence qui jusqu'alors me contentait, je ne le supportais pas. On m'inflige une vieillesse affreuse! me disais-je. La mort semble encore plus inacceptable quand la vie a perdu sa fierté; je n'arrêtais plus d'y penser: à la mienne, à celle de Sartre. En ouvrant les yeux chaque matin je me disais en même temps: Nous allons mourir. Et: Ce monde est horrible. Je faisais des cauchemars chaque nuit. Il y en avait un qui revenait si souvent que j'en ai noté une version:

"Cette nuit, un rêve d'une extrême violence. Je suis avec Sartre dans ce studio; le phono repose sous son voile. Soudain, musique, sans que j'aie bougé. Il y a un disque sur le plateau, il tourne. Je manoeuvre le bouton d'arrêt: impossible de l'arrêter, il tourne de plus en plus vite, l'aiguille ne peut pas suivre, le bras prend d'extraordinaires positions, l'intérieur du phono ronfle comme une chaudière, on voit des espèces de flammes, et le luisant du disque noir, affolé; d'abord l'idée que le phono va se détraquer, une angoisse limitée, puis qui devient immense: TOUT va exploser, une rébellion magique, incompréhensible, c'est un dérèglement de tout. J'ai peur, je suis aux abois; je pense à appeler un spécialiste. Je crois me souvenir qu'il est venu; mais, c'est moi qui finalement ai pensé à déconnecter le phono et j'avais peur en touchant la prise; il s'est arrêté. Quel ravage! le bras réduit à une espèce de brindille tordue, l'aiguille pulvérisée, le disque pulvérisé, le

---

* Rapporté par Benoît Rey dans un excellent et affreux livre: *Les Egorgeurs*.

plateau déjà attaqué, les accessoires anéantis, et la maladie con-
tinuant à couver à l'intérieur de la machine." A l'instant du réveil
où je le récapitulai, ce rêve avait pour moi un sens évident: la
force indocile et mystérieuse, c'était celle du temps, des choses,
elle dévastait mon corps (ce misérable rogaton de bras desséché),
elle mutilait, elle menaçait de radical anéantissement mon passé,
ma vie, tout ce que j'étais.

La Force de choses, pp. 611–612
Force of Circumstance, pp. 584–585

17. Un des traits qui m'a le plus frappé, c'est combien ils ré-
pugnent à mettre en question le monde et eux-mêmes.

L'Amérique au jour le jour, p. 374

18. Ce qui manque d'abord à la femme c'est de faire dans
l'angoisse et l'orgueil l'apprentissage de son délaissement et de sa
transcendance.

Le Deuxième Sexe, p. 555
The Second Sex, p. 711

19. Il y avait une grande gaieté dans cette foule en marche
étonnée de sa liberté. Et comme je me sentais bien! La solitude
est une mort et, en retrouvant la chaleur des contacts humains je
ressuscitais. . . . C'avait été une belle journée qui encourageait à
l'espoir.

La Force des choses, pp. 632–633
Force of Circumstance, pp. 605–606

20. Dix mille Algériens étaient parqués au Vel d'Hiv, comme
autrefois les Juifs à Drancy. De nouveau je détestais tout, ce pays,
moi-même, et le monde. . . . On aurait pu faire sauter l'Acropole et Rome et toute la terre, je n'aurai pas levé un doigt pour
l'empêcher.

La Force des choses, p. 627
Force of Circumstance, p. 599

CHAPTER IX

1. Je m'émus peu. Malgré son infirmité, ma mère était solide.
Et, somme toute, elle avait l'âge de mourir.

Une Mort très douce, pp. 16–17
A Very Easy Death, p. 12

2. Quand je me disais: elle a l'âge de mourir, c'étaient des mots vides, comme tant de mots. Pour la première fois, j'apercevais en elle un cadavre en sursis.

Une Mort très douce, p. 29
A Very Easy Death, p. 20

3. J'imaginais sa détresse. Elle croyait au ciel; mais malgré son âge, ses infirmités, ses malaises, elle était farouchement accrochée à la terre et elle avait de la mort une horreur animale.

Une Mort très douce, p. 27
A Very Easy Death, p. 14

4. . . . Je rangeais des papiers quand le téléphone a sonné. Bost m'appelait de Paris: "votre mère a eu un accident," me dit-il. J'ai pensé: une auto l'a renversée. Elle se hissait péniblement de la chaussée sur le trottoir, appuyée sur sa canne, et une auto l'avait renversée.

Une Mort très douce, p. 11
A Very Easy Death, p. 9

5. C'était une belle journée d'automne, au ciel bleu: je marchais à travers un monde couleur de plomb et je me rendis compte que l'accident de ma mère me frappait beaucoup plus que je ne l'avais prévu. Je ne savais pas trop pourquoi. Il l'avait arraché à son cadre, à son rôle, aux images figées dans lesquelles je l'emprisonnais. Je la reconnaissais dans cette alitée, mais je ne reconnaissais pas la pitié ni l'espèce de désarroi qu'elle suscitait en moi. . . . Quand par la bouche de ma mère c'était cette élite qui parlait, je me hérissais; mais je me sentais solidaire de l'infirme clouée sur ce lit et qui luttait pour faire reculer la paralysie, la mort.

Une Mort très douce, pp. 30–31
A Very Easy Death, pp. 20–22

6. "Mais à quoi bon la tourmenter si elle est perdue? Qu'on la laisse mourir tranquille," me dit Poupette en larmes.

Une Mort très douce, p. 40
A Very Easy Death, p. 27

7. Je suis rentrée chez moi, j'ai causé avec Sartre, nous avons écouté du Bartok. Soudain, à onze heures du soir, crise de larmes qui dégénère presque en crise de nerfs.
Stupeur. Quand mon père est mort je n'ai pas versé un pleur. J'avais dit à ma soeur: "Pour maman, ça sera pareil." Tous mes chagrins, jusqu'à cette nuit, je les avais compris; même quand ils

me submergeaient, je me reconnaissais en eux. Cette fois, mon désespoir échappait à mon contrôle: quelqu'un d'autre que moi pleurait en moi. Je parlai à Sartre de la bouche de ma mère telle que je l'avais vue le matin et de tout ce que j'y déchiffrais: une gloutonnerie refusée, une humilité presque servile, de l'espoir, de la détresse, une solitude—celle de sa mort, celle de sa vie—qui ne voulait pas s'avouer. Et ma propre bouche, m'a-t-il dit, ne m'obéissait plus; j'avais posé celle de maman sur mon visage et j'en imitais malgré moi les mimiques. Toute sa personne, toute son existence s'y matérialisaient et la compassion me déchirait.

Une Mort très douce, pp. 46–47
A Very Easy Death, p. 31

8. (J'ai tenu sans arrêt la main de maman qui me suppliait: ne me laisse pas partir. Elle disait: je ne reverrai pas Simone.) . . .

J'ai demandé au portier de me retenir une place dans l'avion qui décollait le lendemain à dix heures et demie. Des engagements étaient pris, Sartre me conseillait d'attendre un jour ou deux: impossible. Je ne tenais pas particulièrement à revoir maman avant sa mort; mais je ne supportais pas l'idée qu'elle ne me reverrait pas. Pourquoi accorder tant d'importance à un instant, puisqu'il n'y aura pas de mémoire? Il n'y aura pas non plus de réparation. J'ai compris pour mon compte jusque dans la moelle de mes os, que dans les derniers moments d'un moribond on puisse enfermer l'absolu.

Une Mort très douce, pp. 94–95
A Very Easy Death, pp. 62–63

9. Ma vie se déroulait auprès d'elle et n'avait qu'un but: la protéger. . . . Ce qui nous éprouvait surtout, c'étaient les agonies de maman, ses résurrections, et notre propre contradiction. Dans cette course entre la souffrance et la mort, nous souhaitions avec ardeur que celle-ci arrivât la première. Pourtant, quand maman dormait, le visage inanimé, nous épiions anxieusement sur la liseuse blanche le faible movement du ruban noir qui retenait sa montre: la peur du spasme final nous tordait l'estomac.

Une Mort très douce, pp. 112–115
A Very Easy Death, pp. 73–75

10. Ces instants de vaine torture, rien au monde ne pourrait les justifier.

Une Mort très douce, p. 126
A Very Easy Death, p. 81

11. "La seule chose qui me console," m'a-t-elle [Poupette] dit, "c'est que moi aussi je passerai par là. Sans ça, ça serait trop injuste." Oui: nous assistions à la répétition générale de notre propre enterrement. Le malheur c'est que cette aventure commune à tous, chacun la vit seul. Nous n'avions pas quitté maman pendant cette agonie qu'elle confondait avec une convalescence et nous avions été radicalement séparées d'elle.

Une Mort très douce, p. 154
A Very Easy Death, pp. 99–100

12. Il arrive très rarement que l'amour, l'amitié, la camaraderie surmontent la solitude de la mort; malgré les apparences, même lorsque je tenais la main de maman, je n'étais pas seule avec elle: je lui mentais. Parce qu'elle avait toujours été mystifiée, cette suprême mystification m'était odieuse. Je me rendais complice du destin qui lui faisait violence. Pourtant dans chaque cellule de mon corps, je m'unissais à son refus, à sa révolte: c'est pour cela aussi que sa défaite m'a terrassée. Bien que j'aie été absente quand elle a expiré—alors que par trois fois j'avais assisté aux derniers instants d'un agonisant—c'est à son chevet que j'ai vu la Mort des danses macabres, grimaçante et narquoise, la Mort des contes de veillée qui frappe à la porte, une faux à la main, la Mort qui vient d'ailleurs, étrangère, inhumaine: elle avait le visage même de maman découvrant sa mâchoire dans un grand sourire d'ignorance.

Une Mort très douce, pp. 162–163
A Very Easy Death, p. 105

CHAPTER X

1. "Simone de Beauvoir, an Interview," by Madeleine Gobeil, translated by Bernard Frechtmann. *The Paris Review*. No. 34, Spring–Summer 1965, p. 29.

2. *Ibid.*, pp. 36–38.

3. Je pleurai sur sa mort [celle de Maggie Tulliver dans *Le Moulin sur la Floss*] pendant des heures. Les autres la condamnaient parce qu'elle valait mieux qu'eux; je lui ressemblais, et je vis désormais dans mon isolement non une marque d'infamie mais un signe d'élection. Je n'envisageais pas d'en mourir. A travers son héroïne, je m'identifiais à l'auteur; un jour une adolescente, une

autre moi-même, tremperait de ses larmes un roman où j'aurais raconté ma propre histoire.

Mémoires d'une jeune fille rangée, p. 141
Memoirs of a Dutiful Daughter, p. 148

4. Soudain je devenais une pierre, l'acier la fendait: c'est l'enfer.

La Force des choses, p. 143
Force of Circumstance, p. 128

5. Son corps est de pierre, elle voudrait hurler; mais la pierre n'a pas de voix; ni de larmes.

Les Belles Images, p. 247
Les Belles Images, p. 216

6. Je m'y abandonnais [au remords et à la peur] selon un rythme qui depuis ma petite enfance a réglé à peu près toute ma vie. Je traversais des semaines d'euphorie; et puis, pendant quelques heures, une tornade me dévastait, elle saccageait tout. Pour mieux mériter mon désespoir, je roulais dans les abîmes de la mort, de l'infini, du néant. Je n'ai jamais su, quand le ciel redevenait calme, si je m'éveillais d'un cauchemar ou si je retombais dans un long rêve bleu.

La Force de l'âge, p. 70
The Prime of Life, p. 57

7. Je pense aujourd'hui que, dans la condition qui est la mienne, la vie enveloppe deux vérités contre lesquelles il n'y a pas à choisir et qu'il faut affronter ensemble; la gaieté d'exister et l'horreur de finir. Mais alors je basculais de l'une à l'autre. La seconde ne l'emportait que par brefs éclairs mais je la soupçonnais d'être la plus valable.

La Force de l'âge, p. 215
The Prime of Life, p. 168

8. "Les choses n'ont jamais tant d'importance; elles changent, elles finissent, et surtout au bout du compte tout le monde meurt: ça arrange tout."

"Ah! ça, c'est juste une façon de fuir les problèmes," dit Robert.

Je l'arrêtai: "A moins que les problèmes ne soient une façon de fuir la vérité. Evidemment," ajoutai-je, "quand on a décidé que c'est la vie qui est vraie, l'idée de la mort semble une fuite. Mais réciproquement . . ."

Robert secoua la tête: "Il y a une différence. On prouve qu'on a choisi de croire à la vie en vivant; si on croit sincèrement que la mort seule est vraie, on devrait se tuer. En fait, même les suicides n'ont jamais ce sens-là."

"Ça peut être parce qu'on est étourdi et lâche qu'on continue à vivre," dis-je. "C'est le plus facile. Mais ça ne prouve rien non plus."

"D'abord c'est important que le suicide soit difficile," dit Robert. "Et puis continuer à vivre, ce n'est pas seulement continuer à respirer. Personne ne réussit à s'installer dans l'indifférence. Tu aimes des choses, tu en détestes d'autres, tu t'indignes, tu admires: ça implique que tu reconnais les valeurs de la vie." Il sourit: "Je suis tranquille. Nous n'avons pas fini de discuter sur les camps, sur tout le reste. Tu te sentes impuissante, comme moi, comme tout le monde, devant certains faits qui t'accablent, alors tu te réfugies dans un scepticisme généralisé: mais ce n'est pas sérieux."

Je ne répondis rien. Evidemment, demain je discuterais de nouveau sur un tas de choses: ça prouvait-il qu'elles cesseraient de me paraître insignifiantes? et si oui, c'est peut-être que je recommencerais à me faire duper.

Les Mandarins, p. 337
The Mandarins, pp. 359–360

9. J'ai pensé dans un éclair: "Robert a bien raison. Ça n'existe pas, l'indifférence. . . . Oui, c'est par fatigue, par paresse, par honte de mon ignorance que j'avais bêtement prétendu le contraire."

Les Mandarins, p. 343
The Mandarins, p. 366

10. La littérature apparaît lorsque quelque chose dans la vie se dérègle; pour écrire—Blanchot l'a bien montré dans le paradoxe d'Aytré—la première condition c'est que la réalité cesse d'*aller de soi*; alors seulement on est capable de la voir et de la donner à voir. . . . Mes consignes de travail demeurèrent creuses jusqu'au jour où une menace pesa sur lui et où je retrouvai dans l'anxiété une certaine solitude. La mésaventure du trio fit beaucoup plus que me fournir un sujet de roman: elle me donna la possibilité de le traiter.

La Force de l'âge, p. 374
The Prime of Life, p. 290

11. Calme indifférence.

L'Invitée, p. 209
She Came to Stay, p. 191

12. Est-ce qu'elle était devenue n'importe qui? Était-ce pour cela qu'elle se trouvait si légère, délivrée d'elle-même et de toute son escorte étouffante de joies et de soucis? Elle ferma les yeux; sans secousse la voiture roulait et le temps glissait.

L'Invitée, p. 195
She Came to Stay, p. 179

13. N'importe quoi pouvait donc m'arriver, comme à n'importe qui: quelle révolution!

La Force de l'âge, p. 300
The Prime of Life, p. 233

14. Dans le plus mauvais des cas je pouvais compter sur environ douze ans de vie; d'ici douze ans, la bombe atomique nous aurait tous liquidés.

La Force des choses, p. 277
Force of Circumstance, p. 257

15. . . . Des anges me berçaient . . . émerveillée de me retrouver intacte et sauvée de la peur.

La Force des choses, p. 277
Force of Circumstance, p. 258

16. . . . Le visage poilu de Lucienne Baudin, son agonie . . . l'ablation du sein . . . les compagnes de chambre de Lucienne: dix ans après l'autre sein prend, on meurt dans d'affreuses douleurs.

La Force des choses, p. 276
Force of Circumstance, p. 257

17. Eh bien voilà! me dis-je. Ça arrive; ça arrive: c'est fini!

La Force de l'âge, p. 310
The Prime of Life, p. 241

18. . . . D'avoir éprouvé si peu d'émotion quand j'avais cru frôler la mort.

La Force de l'âge, p. 310
The Prime of Life, p. 241

19. C'est donc ça la mort! Et je mourus.

La Force de l'âge, p. 509
The Prime of Life, p. 393

20. Ce que de toutes mes forces je refusais, c'était l'horreur de cette nuit qui ne serait jamais horrible puisqu'elle ne serait pas, mais qui était horrible pour moi qui existais; je tolérais mal de me sentir éphémère, finie, une goutte d'eau dans l'océan; par moments, toutes mes entreprises m'apparaissaient comme vaines, le bonheur devenait un leurre et le monde le masque dérisoire du néant.

La Force de l'âge, p. 616
The Prime of Life, p. 475

21. D'après les témoignages que j'ai recueillis, la peur de la mort n'est généralement pas l'envers d'un ardent amour pour la vie: au contraire. "La mort était mon vertige parce que je n'aimais pas la vie," écrit Sartre en parlant de son enfance. De même que les parents, les époux anxieux ne sont pas ceux qui aiment le plus, mais ceux qui éprouvent un manque au coeur de leurs sentiments, les gens mal à l'aise dans leur peau sont ceux qui ruminent le plus assidûment leur mort. Et il ne faut pas croire que ceux qui—comme Lamartine—l'appellent à cor et à cri la désirent vraiment: en en parlant sans cesse, ils manifestent seulement qu'elle les obsède.

La Vieillesse, p. 469

22. "Un révolver c'est solide, c'est en acier, c'est un objet. Se heurter enfin à l'objet" écrit Drieu à la fin du *Feu follet*. Il nous livre ici la raison profonde de la fascination que la mort exerce sur l'homme de droite; elle est le seul événement *réel* qui puisse se produire du sein d'une vie repliée sur sa propre immanence, d'une vie sans contenu. Coupé du monde, coupé de semblables qui lui sont tous étrangers, sans amour, sans but, l'homme de droite est enfermé dans une subjectivité vide, où rien ne se passe qu'en idée; seule la mort lui *arrive* tout en lui demeurant intérieur; absolument solitaire, sans relation avec autrui, sans objet, sans avenir, elle réalise la radicale séparation. On meurt seul. Voilà pourquoi l'homme de droite décide de voir dans la mort la vérité de la vie; elle lui confirme que chacun vit seul, séparé; à sa lumière je ne relève plus que de moi; ce moi est étranger à tous ceux qui sont étrangers à ma mort; à tous. . . . La méditation de la mort est la suprême sagesse de ceux qui sont déjà des morts.

"La Pensée de droite aujourd'hui," in *Privilèges*, pp. 193–194

Index

ABOUT THE AUTHOR

Elaine Marks has degrees from Bryn Mawr College and the University of Pennsylvania; she received her doctorate from New York University, where she taught nine years, with time off as a Fulbright Scholar in Paris. She held a Junior Fellowship at the Institute for Research in the Humanities in Madison, Wisconsin, and taught five years at the University of Wisconsin. She is now Professor of French at the University of Massachusetts. Her publications include *Colette* (1960), *French Poetry from Baudelaire to the Present* (1962), three textbooks, and various articles and reviews.

The text of this book was set in Janson-Linotype and printed by offset on P & S Special Book manufactured by P. H. Glatfelter Co., Spring Grove, Pa. Composed, printed and bound by Quinn & Boden Company, Inc., Rahway, N.J.